THE HOUSES OF OLD
CUBA

Jean-Luc de Laguarigue would particularly like to thank
Isabelle Camard for her help with the photography.

THE HOUSES OF OLD
CUBA

Llilian Llanes
Photography by Jean-Luc de Laguarigue

Thames & Hudson

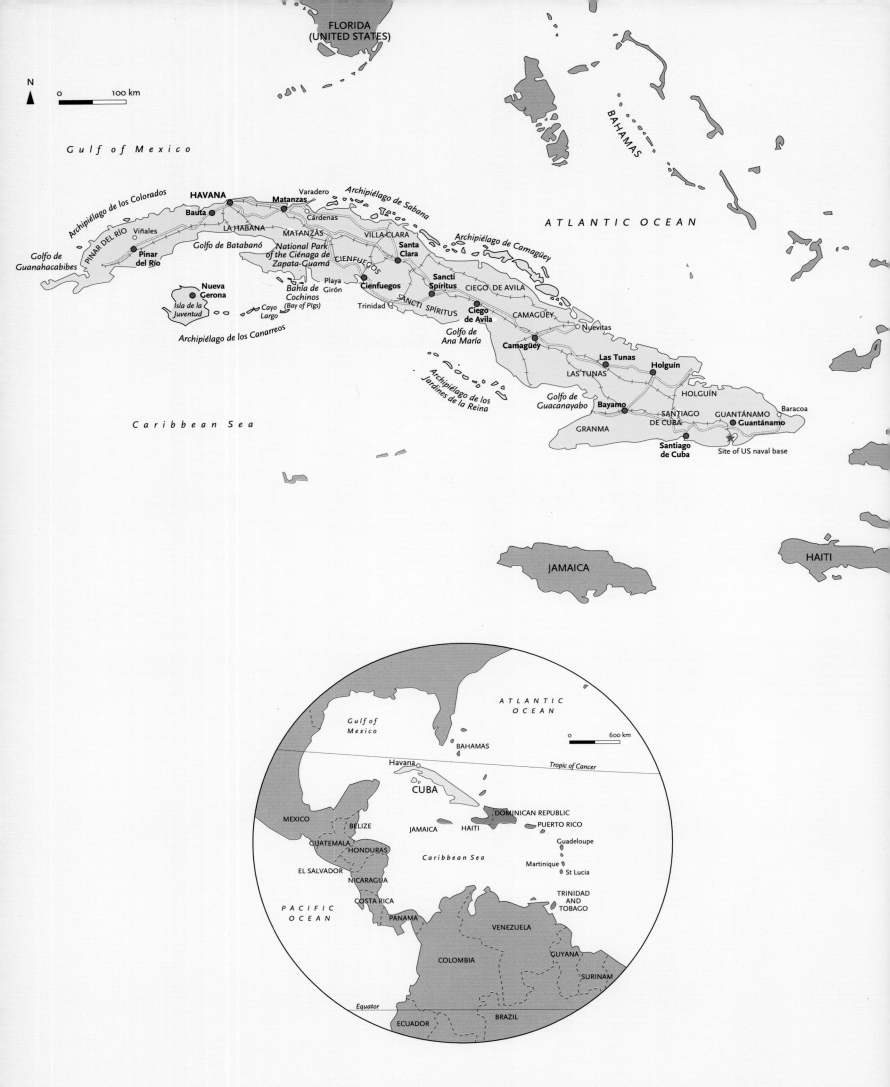

Contents

From cabin to mansion

The evolution of Cuba's architecture reflects the island's overall development. The houses provide an insight into periods of greater or lesser prosperity, mirroring the social inequalities that have always existed as well as indicating some of the gradual changes in customs and ways of life. There are striking differences between the houses built in the capital and those in all the other towns and villages, resulting from Havana's considerably greater rate of growth by comparison with the rest of the country. Both the economic and social contexts of the relevant period must be taken into account when looking at Cuban houses. In particular, the relative insecurity of life in the provinces compared with the capital is a crucial factor. Almost as soon as Havana had become the most important town on the island, the way in which it developed set it apart from the rest of the country. The families in the capital were the most wealthy and enjoyed many material advantages which were rarely available to those living elsewhere. Outlying districts remained isolated for a long time and depended to a large extent on the many foreigners – pirates, privateers or ordinary merchants – who landed on their shores and exchanged a variety of goods with the local inhabitants.

Havana was expected to take the lead, and at every period of the island's history was regarded as an example to be followed by the rich families in the provinces. In all the towns of any size the type of houses built in

Archway and patio in the Palacio
del Segundo Cabo, Havana.

Havana were copied on a local scale. On the whole, they were less ambitiously planned than those in the capital, although some built by wealthy families rivalled them in elegance and grandeur. Several houses still standing in the town of Trinidad, and in Camagüey and Santiago, for example, are proof of the existence of a Creole oligarchy with settled customs and traditions, whose members enjoyed a way of life in keeping with their status. People such as these were not always willing to concede Havana's claims to superiority. The Creole oligarchy which established itself in the inland regions of the country played a crucial role in the emergence of the Cuban nation. At certain periods the educated people in these areas were particularly influential, and in many spheres were acknowledged members of the country's avant-garde.

The architecture of the capital was an obvious influence on building elsewhere, although in certain places individual characteristics emerged to challenge the generally imitative style adopted in the countryside. The villages in the interior were influenced by Havana, which in turn absorbed influences from abroad. Local custom had an impact on the methods and style of the builders who, through a long process of adaptation to their environment, were responsible for the evolution of the very individual character of the Cuban house.

Opposite: Wickets cut into the front doors help to ventilate the house and maintain contact with neighbours without compromising privacy.

Right: There are only two seasons in Cuba – the dry season and the rainy season. Scenes such as this are typical of the *mal tiempo*, when it rains constantly.

Below right: The palm tree can resist the strongest winds and appears on Cuba's national coat of arms. It became the symbol of the struggle for independence and poets writing in praise of their country have been inspired by it as an image:

Pero del mundo vegetal señora
y del índico suelo timbre y gala
es la palma, que siempre vencedora
en llanos y colinas se señala;
es del campo deidad encantadora
de la luz, al bajar, primer escala,
florero del agreste pavimento,
trono sin rey, silvestre monumento.

(Queen of the flora and graceful and elegant creation of the soil of the Indies, the palm, always triumphant, stands out on plains and hills. It is the bewitching spirit of the countryside, the first to be touched by each day's light, essence of the rural earth, a throne without a king, a sylvan monument.)

Federico García Copley,
'La vuelta al campo'.

The island of Cuba

Gateway to the West Indies

Cuba is the biggest of the islands of the West Indies. With an average width of one hundred kilometres, it has a land surface covering more than 100,000 square kilometres. Its geographically strategic position at the entrance to the Gulf of Mexico has been a determining factor in the history of the island since the beginning of its conquest by Spain. Cuba was the main staging post for ships between the Old World and the New, and as such its possession was regarded as vital for the maintenance of control over the entire West Indies. Its very irregular coastline has a great number of harbours, bays and beaches, which in the past were an essential element in the economy and politics of the country. The fame of its great ports, the beauty and fertility of the land, as well as its strategic position in the Caribbean, made Cuba the queen of the seas for a large part of the colonial era. The Spanish monarchy invested a great deal in the security of the ports, and built extensive fortifications to ensure their defence. The country's mainly agricultural economy was in the colonial era based on sugar-cane, tobacco, coffee and cattle rearing. Today some of these still form a significant element of Cuba's wealth. The production of nickel (now one of the most important industries), citrus fruit, tourism and the promising new area of biotechnology are other factors which play a major role in the modern economy.

The island's landscape is not particularly varied. Its few rivers do not flow fast and are relatively shallow. The land is generally low-lying, only a quarter of it being mountainous. Hilly regions include the Cordillera de Guaniguanico, the Sierra de Trinidad, the Sierra Sancti Spíritus, the Sierra Cristal and the Sierra Maestra, where the 1,974-metre-high Pico Turquino towers up as the highest point on the island. The rest of the country consists of swampy areas and the plains where the greater part of the population lives and where most of the economic activity is based.[1] The Cuban population is mainly of mixed race and, in contrast with other Latin-American countries, the indigenous people have mostly disappeared. The first inhabitants of Cuba were virtually eliminated when the Spaniards conquered and colonized the island. However, the need for a subject workforce to compensate for the slaughtered Indian population led to

The sea is in the country's soul and has inspired some fine poets:

El mar canta canciones de espuma
toca marchas triunfales de olas;
y en azules bataholas
llena de cantante bruma
la terquedad de la sirte.
La sirte, mar armonioso,
duerme, no quiere ni oírte.
¡Es tan fecundo el reposo!

(The sea sings songs of foam, plays triumphal marches with the waves; and this blue uproar full of the song of the spray meets with the harshness of the sandbank. Harmonious sea, the sandbank is sleeping and has no desire to hear you. Rest itself is reward enough!)

Regino Boti, 'La sirte',
from *El mar y la montaña*.

A road across the mountains in the east of the country.

La montaña, ¿cómo es bella
la montaña?
¿cuando es azul lejanía,
cuando encendiendo sus entrañas
luminares la noche
y en verdores vibra el día?

La montaña, ¿cómo es bella
la montaña?
Es bella desde su entraña,
y hecha azul lejanía,
cuando la noche es estrellas
y en flores se desentraña,
la verde gama del día.

(Where does the mountain's beauty come from?
Is it most beautiful when it is blue in the distance,
or illuminated by its glowing heart at night, or
vibrant with green by day? Where does the mountain's
beauty come from? It is beautiful to its very core
when it is blue in the distance and when the
night blossoms with stars, and when with flowers
unravels the green palette of daylight.)

Regino Boti, 'La montaña', from *El mar y la montaña*.

the introduction of black slaves, mainly brought by the French and English from Africa, although they sometimes came from neighbouring islands such as Jamaica.

For a long time, therefore, the growth of Cuba's population was a direct result of the introduction of black slaves, the arrival of Spanish immigrants and the interbreeding between the white settlers and the blacks from Africa. In contrast with other European colonists, the Spaniards mixed readily with the slaves, creating a predominantly mulatto population and a hybrid culture receptive to all kinds of influences. Gradually people of other European nationalities or from other parts of the world came in varying numbers to join the Spaniards, and in their own individual way became absorbed in the life of the island. A notable impact was made in the eighteenth century by the arrival of the French fleeing the revolution in the neighbouring island of Haiti, and later by the Chinese who replaced the black slaves in certain areas of work,

Above: Portrait of a Cuban in the town of Trinidad. The number of Spanish immigrants in Cuba greatly increased in the late nineteenth century after the end of the Spanish–Cuban war. There are still many direct descendants of the Spaniards who came in their thousands to make a new life on the island.

Opposite: Direct descendants of the first Africans to arrive on the island still live in many of the towns, as here in Trinidad. They have played a major part in the creation of the Cuban culture and identity.

when the slave trade and the use of slaves finally came to an end. The increase in commercial output during the island's colonial history led to the arrival and integration of immigrants of diverse origins, who were to put their own individual stamp on the national culture.

Inevitably, certain features which are characteristic of the Cuban population today are a direct result of the country's origins, and of the way the colony developed after the Spaniards realized that there were few lucrative resources to exploit on the island. The whites from Europe, the blacks from Africa and the other groups, who all came to Cuba for different reasons, were obliged to adapt to the country's circumstances, and all played a part in the creation of a uniquely Cuban culture.

However, it must also be recognized that because of the discrimination which accompanied the institution of slavery (which was abolished only in the nineteenth century) the cultural contribution of the blacks was belittled, and for a long time attempts were made to ignore the role of the Africans in the emergence of Cuban culture. In his celebrated anthology *Sóngoro Cosongo* (first published in 1931) the Cuban poet Nicolás Guillén drew attention to this situation. He referred to it particularly clearly, with both truth and humour, in the poem entitled 'La canción del bongó':[2]

En esta tierra mulata
de africano y español
(Santa Bárbara de un lado,
del otro lado Changó)
siempre falta algún abuelo,
cuando no sobra algún don
y hay títulos de Castilla
con parientes de Bondó:
vale más callarse amigos
y no menear la cuestión,
porque venimos de lejos
y andamos de dos en dos.

(In this land, made mulatto by African and Spaniard, with Santa Barbara on one side, and Changó on the other, there is always an ancestor missing, when there isn't a *don* too many, there are some with titles from Castile, and relations from Bondó: friends, it's better to keep quiet and not bring the matter up, as we all come from far away, and walk along two by two.)

The legacy of the Indians

The process of conquest and colonization of the island of Cuba, 'discovered' by Christopher Columbus in October 1492, did not begin until early in the sixteenth century. It was undertaken by the Spaniard Diego Velázquez, who became the colony's first governor. Velázquez crushed the resistance of the few Indians inhabiting the island, who virtually disappeared within a very few years as a result of the violent, merciless onslaught by the Spaniards.

According to the conquistadors' own accounts, these original inhabitants were very peaceable. They generally wore no clothes, apart from the married women, who wore cotton skirts which covered them from the waist to the knees. As a pro-

Opposite: Families in Trinidad have traditionally prepared in their own homes the church's statues to be used in processions. In some cases this task has passed from generation to generation of the same family.

Below: Part of the first school building in Trinidad can still be seen in Calle San José, one of the oldest streets in the town. Cuban children have always enjoyed walking barefoot in the street during the rainy season.

tection against the sun, the wind and mosquitoes they greased their bodies, and decorated themselves with designs of a symbolic and magical significance. They lived together in very primitive huts called *bohíos*, big enough to accommodate a large number of people. These wooden cabins had roofs thatched with palm leaves, secured from top to bottom with lianas. These strong and durable materials were used largely because they were readily available in the countryside and because they kept out both the rain and the intense heat of the sun. They were in fact cooler than the houses with tiled roofs that were built at a later period. Wealthy families soon began to build in brick, and substituted tiles for natural materials such as straw. However, the old wooden huts, one of the last links with the indigenous population, continued to be built throughout the colonial period. They were, unfortunately, vulnerable to fire and were eventually relegated to the country areas and used by only the poorest in both towns and villages.

Contemporary eye-witness accounts describe how the indigenous people squatted on the ground in their huts, which contained nothing apart from cooking implements. Only a few 'caciques' or chiefs sometimes possessed a carved chair in their dwellings. Fashioned from a single piece of wood, the chair was made in the shape of an animal with eyes and ears of gold, short legs and a raised tail. Use of the chair was the prerogative of the cacique or the *behíque* (a kind of witch doctor, who healed by blowing on his patient and by speaking mysterious, almost inaudible, words).[3]

People slept in hammocks made from fibres tied together at each end, and attached to the upright timbers of the house. The Spaniards were intrigued by the Indians' habit of carrying smouldering charcoal to perfume the air – this must have been the origin of the Creole custom of using embers rather than matches to light cigars at table, because they preferred the smell.

The indigenous people roasted roots and tubers for their food. From contemporary

evidence we know that, among other things, they cultivated manioc (used by the Spaniards to make cassava, which in the early days was a substitute for bread). They also fished from wooden boats, dug out of a single piece of wood with flints and capable of carrying up to fifty people. They ate their fish almost raw, and a variety of other small creatures, such as spiders, worms, small lizards (most of them caught by hand), as well as iguanas, grass snakes and agoutis – little rat-like animals which feed on grass and fruits, and whose flesh is said to be delicious. The other important contribution made to the national culture by the original inhabitants is the *ajiaco*. This was a sort of stock in which all kinds of vegetables and animals were cooked. Apart from a few small changes, it remains one of Cuba's specialities.[4]

Opposite: Whites, blacks and mixed-race inhabitants with varying skin colour have always intermarried, giving the Cuban population its present characteristic diversity.

Above: Landscape on the plains near Baracoa.

Overleaf: Almost from the beginning of the colonial period Havana was the most important town on the island, on account of its sheltered port and its strategic position at the mouth of the Gulf of Mexico. The sea-front boulevard, El Malecón, seen here, extends for several kilometres.

A haven for the conquistadors and the first settlers

The island's resources

The colonizers established their first settlements either on the coast or in the areas where the indigenous people were already living, so that they could make use of their labour. The first towns to be built were Baracoa, San Salvador de Bayamo, Santiago de Cuba, San Cristóbal de la Habana (as Havana was first called), Sancti Spíritus, Trinidad and Puerto Príncipe (now Camagüey). These towns all developed in their own way over the years, but are relatively unchanged today. During the first centuries of the colonial period, only Havana, whose initial location was changed, increased appreciably in size. Despite being the seat of an archbishop Baracoa quickly became a backwater – probably because of the inconvenience of its port (although its setting makes it a very attractive town today). Santiago de Cuba, surrounded by mining areas and with a good harbour, soon became as a result the most important town. Its strategic position in the Caribbean Sea was a major factor in its development. Most of Cuba's maritime trade was concentrated in the

Trinidad was founded in 1514 by Diego Velázquez with the intention of exploiting the gold deposits in the area. It lies in the middle of the island, at the foot of the Guamuhaya mountains and a few kilometres from the sea. Today it is primarily an agricultural town. Trinidad was declared a World Heritage Site in 1988 on account of its architectural significance. The mansions built in the eighteenth century for the sugar-cane planters are particularly important in this respect.

extreme south of the island, and expeditions to conquer American mainland territory set out from there. Trading arrangements were entered into with neighbouring colonies.

The arrival of new settlers, meanwhile, meant that the crops cultivated by the local population rapidly became inadequate to meet the growing needs of those who had come to live in the first villages. The Spaniards soon began to rear cattle, introducing cows, horses and pigs, both for use in husbandry and for consumption. It is said that Hernán Cortés was the first person in Cuba – at Baracoa – to rear cows, goats and mares. Later, sugar-cane was introduced and tobacco, already known to the Indians, began to be developed as a crop.

The conquistadors had come to Cuba expecting that they would quickly make their fortune with discoveries of gold and other precious materials, and then return to Spain. But the amount of gold available fell far short of their expectations and, once the prospect of stripping the island of its resources had evaporated, the colonizers had to find other things to do. Those who still had ambitions continued on their way to the American mainland. Others gave up, deciding to remain on the island and accept life in a subsistence economy based on satisfying simple daily requirements. They not only needed to produce their own food, but had to find ways of obtaining other goods they wanted such as wine, oil and flour, which they were obliged to import and exchange for other commodities.

Santiago was the town which expanded most quickly. It was the starting point, among others, for both Hernán Cortés' expeditions of discovery and conquest in Mexico, but its importance gradually diminished after the rich empires on the American continent had been discovered. The Spaniards diverted their attention to the mainland, and the island of Cuba became no more than a stopping place on the way to new conquests. In addition, when the Old Bahama Channel was discovered, the northern part of the island displaced the south in importance, and the bay of Havana, with its superb natural harbour, became an essential port of call for ships sailing between America and Spain. San Cristóbal – later renamed La Habana (Havana) – moved from the south coast to the north, and became, on its new site, the principal town of the island. The governor of Cuba himself went to live there, although Santiago remained the seat of government.

The emigration of some of the first settlers to the American mainland, after the conquistadors had led the way, considerably slowed down the development of the other towns in Cuba, which continued to be underpopulated during the sixteenth century. However, in spite of the uncertainties typical of colonial life at this period, the villages enjoyed relative growth. Their inhabitants managed to provide themselves with the few comforts available at the time, and laid the foundations of a distinctive culture. At about the same period the first groups of African slaves were brought to the island to replace the massacred Indian population. This supply of cheap labour, the basis of the ethnic mix so characteristic of colonial society, was increased to keep pace with the intensification in the production of the colony's principal crops, sugar and coffee. A Creole, mixed-race population was to emerge from this blending of people of different origins – one that was wholly identified with the island and which later provided the foundation on which the Cuban nation was built.

The supremacy of Havana

The population of Havana began to grow significantly after 1555, when the little town of San Cristóbal was destroyed by the French privateer Jacques de Sores. It was rebuilt and renamed, as we have seen, and from then on attempts were made to turn it into a well-defended haven, able to accommodate the fleet of ships that sailed regularly between Cuba and Spain. Sometimes the ships stayed several months, causing an influx of thousands of travellers of many different origins, who swarmed through the streets of the town. Not surprisingly, the first buildings were fortifications designed to protect the territory. In the second half of the sixteenth century, the small *castillo* so easily destroyed by de Sores was replaced by the Castillo de la Real Fuerza. The Castillo del Morro and the Castillo de la Punta were built to protect the bay where the ships were moored – which was more important even than the protection of the town. The long time which the ships spent in port ensured that Havana was in much closer touch with events in Europe than the other settlements and this was one of the factors contributing to its status as the island's most important town. It maintained its dominance over the inland areas of the country for a long time, creating marked contrasts between them. In the areas which remained isolated and with only occasional contact with the capital, the inhabitants even found themselves obliged to resort to practices on the borderline of legality in order to survive. An extensive clandestine trade in a variety of goods grew up among neighbours, both friends and enemies.

Havana: a port first and foremost

Throughout the sixteenth century circumstances were extremely favourable for Havana. At the end of the century the town was being described as beautiful, well-populated, rich and powerful. Protected

This little hamlet of *bohíos* in the Baracoa region at the eastern end of the island calls to mind the layout of the settlement of the original inhabitants. It lies at the foot of a mountain range with a completely flat summit, known as the Yunque ('anvil') of Baracoa.

by the encircling bay, it was considered to be a safe, convenient and well-managed port. Although as Havana was developed it acquired a certain notoriety, it is likely that this reputation was somewhat exaggerated by its contrast with the relative backwardness of the poorer and smaller towns and villages. As on the rest of the island, the inhabitants of Havana in the sixteenth century fell into very contrasting categories: the white settlers, the African blacks and the few Indian survivors, who lived in the neighbouring village of Guanabacoa. The whites were landowners, craftsmen or officials of the colonial administration. However, the homes of these *señores* were far from being large and luxurious. They were relatively restricted in size, the slaves living outside in *bohíos*, as the free blacks did. The poor whites did not enjoy significantly better conditions.

There were a great number of relatively comfortable small houses made of wood and palm leaves in Havana, and a few buildings constructed of less perishable materials. The population was defined by arbitrary social criteria, but lived all together in the centre of the town. The blacks, those of mixed race and the poor whites lived side by side with the newly evolving oligarchy, and all joined forces without question when they needed to defend the town in the face of an imminent enemy attack.

In those days the streets of Havana were already full of hawkers offering their wares from door to door. The blacks carried beef and pork for sale on big trays, and the whites sold fish. As well as this thriving street trade, there were also small shops, taverns, inns and all kinds of other attractions for the large number of visitors who stayed in the town. Although the presence of a fleet of ships gave the city a bad reputation and was a dubious social influence, it was also of great advantage to the inhabitants, who made money from the sometimes prolonged stays of the thousands of visitors thronging the town. In exchange for essential goods, they sold their own produce to the ships' crews (such as salt beef, fruit, fats, water and wood). The ships' passengers took lodgings with the local people, and spent their money freely – mostly on gambling, an increasingly popular practice which was the cause of frequent brawls in the streets of Havana.

The house as a place of safety in the sixteenth century

There are few sixteenth-century buildings still standing in the first towns built by the conquistadors, and little useful evidence remains from a period in which the main preoccupation was simple survival in difficult conditions. When he settled at Santiago de Cuba, Diego Velázquez did, however, build himself a house using relatively

hard-wearing materials. Although it has been much altered over the years, expert research has been able to identify the conquistador's house. It stands in the city's main square, and has now been restored. There is, however, almost no trace of the dwellings of the earliest inhabitants in the other towns, since the building materials used were so impermanent. With the exception of the provincial capitals, the inhabitants of the small towns in the interior generally lived in clusters of *bohíos* near their enclosed fields and the land on which they cultivated crops for their own use and for sale, both legally and illegally.

These villages amounted to little more than places where families grouped together to protect themselves as best they could. It is clear that the first Spanish settlers in Cuba lived in much the same modest conditions and took as their model the indigenous *bohío*. The existence of large numbers of these huts made of wood and palm leaves prompted the Cuban historian Joaquín Weiss to label the sixteenth century the *bohío* century.

Fortunately a few buildings in Havana have survived to give us an idea of what a typical dwelling of the period was like. Thanks to documents which have been preserved, we know that most houses were small, with walls of *yagua* (a type of palm tree) or earth, and roofs of palm leaves. Very few houses from this early period have been found with stone walls and tiled roofs, although their simple construction did not require any great degree of building

Opposite and above: The *bohío* or cabin is the oldest kind of dwelling in Cuba and can still be found in other parts of the Caribbean. It is built with various organic materials, such as pieces of wood, leaves and tree trunks. Leaves from the various different kinds of palm tree growing on the island have always been used for the roof. Today cabins like these can be seen near Baracoa.

skill. Stone (specifically from Jaimanita) was not widely used for houses until later. The island's simple craftsmen built these first houses – still small, low and with thick walls – for the handful of families who formed the local ruling class. As a rule they were strongly influenced by the style of houses of southern Spain, and in particular by the Moorish buildings so common in that region. It must not be forgotten that from the very beginning the island was in particularly close contact with the port of Seville, which was the point of departure for most of the emigrants coming to settle in the colony. Although the builders and their craftsmen often had only a basic knowledge of popular Andalusian architecture and the *mudéjar* style which was particularly in favour at the time, many typically Andalusian features reached Cuba, where they were suitably modified. The type of building was adapted to the local climate and to the demands of life in the tropics. The builders had to use the materials to hand on the island, wood being the most readily available. The abundance of dense woodland throughout the island meant that timber was the building material most often used by the early settlers. The variety of wood of exceptional quality was renowned well beyond Cuba. From the sixteenth century onwards it was even used in Spain – the Escorial Palace was built using magnificent mahogany, ebony, gaïac and ironwood that had been brought from Cuba. With the passing of time, Cuban houses grew bigger, were more open towards the street and became more individual through the use of increasingly sophisticated architectural and decorative elements. But the precarious conditions in which the early settlers found themselves meant that the primary function of their home was a protective one.

House at the corner of Calle Teniente Rey and Calle Bernaza in the old part of Havana. Close by is a square containing the church of Santo Cristo del Buen Viaje, where sailors used to go to pray before joining their ships. This low-built, compact little house, with its thick walls and *cuarto esquinero* or corner room, is one of the oldest in Havana and probably dates from the sixteenth century. Today it is used as a restaurant.

Above: Peasant homes in Trinidad.

Right: A *bohío* at Baracoa.

Opposite: The Casa de los Pimienta, No. 4 Calle Tacón, in old Havana, belonged to José Díaz Pimienta. It dates from the seventeenth century, but was later rebuilt. Unusually for the time, it had a mezzanine floor, but retained the horizontal shape of seventeenth-century houses.

Right: This memorial stone marks the spot where Doña María de Cepero y Nieto, a member of the Havana aristocracy, was mortally wounded in 1557. The story goes that she was accidentally shot as she prayed in the Parroquial Mayor, which was partly situated on the site now occupied by the Municipal Museum, in the old Palacio de los Capitanes Generales.

Below right: With its thick walls, tiled roof, few windows and small rooms, this house on the corner of Calle Obrapía and Calle Compostela in old Havana is typical of smaller houses dating from the beginning of the seventeenth century.

An architecture for the tropics

An insecure way of life

At the beginning of the seventeenth century Santiago and Havana were still the island's most important towns. The notorious Dutch pirate Esquemeling described in detail the complexities of the trading that took place in the Caribbean Sea, involving tobacco, skins and logwood (Campeachy wood). His memoirs provide a fascinating insight into the lives of the island's inhabitants, and the ways in which they were affected by the presence of adventurers of various kinds who were the scourge of the region.

The people of Cuba often had to deal with the pirates, privateers and other rogues living in the Caribbean islands, but could never be sure whether they were coming to trade with them or to launch an attack. Owing to the state of insecurity in which they frequently found themselves, it is understandable that the building of permanent settlements was slow to develop. Houses were in constant danger of destruction during attacks by bandits, as well as being threatened by frequent fires, hurricanes and earth tremors (which occurred mostly in the eastern part of the island). In spite of these difficulties some of the towns in the interior managed to achieve a stable development. One of these was Camagüey, then called Puerto Príncipe, a town with some fine houses. Its wealth, like that of Havana, attracted the attention of the pirate raiders. In this case the new-found riches had been acquired through trade in leather and cattle. Esquemeling recorded that when the pirate Henry Morgan was preparing to attack Havana and explained the benefits of the enterprise to his men 'one of them suggested attacking the town of Puerto Príncipe, declaring that he knew it well, and that because it was far away from the sea and had never been pillaged its inhabitants must be very rich'.[5] It is certainly true that Puerto Príncipe and Trinidad began to see their economies improving as a result of deals they had made with smugglers from Jamaica, which had been in English hands since 1655. This illicit trade allowed them to produce and export sugar, beef cattle and horses so profitably that towards the end of the seventeenth century they were rich enough to whet the appetite of men like Morgan.

Without wanting to minimize the relative progress enjoyed by these towns, it must be said that most of the buildings of this period were not in the same category as those in Havana. Although some houses in Camagüey and Trinidad were noticeably more solidly built, they were all too few in number and did not survive wars and the ravages of time. The unsettled living conditions endured by the inhabitants throughout the seventeenth century meant that their homes were vulnerable on many counts. In a period when onslaughts by pirates on all the coastal regions of Spanish America were relentlessly increasing, those who were unable to defend themselves lived in permanent fear of attack.

The advantages of life in Havana

It was at this time that Havana's defences were strengthened. The port itself was already protected, but now other fortresses and great towers were built in addition. However the town remained accessible from the landward side, which was a continual source of anxiety to the inhabitants. Massive walls were eventually built around the city, but not so as to prevent further expansion in the future.

In spite of the controlled development of Havana within the limits imposed by the sea and the ramparts, the streets were always dirty and badly laid out and maintained. The area which later became the Plaza de la Catedral still flooded in the summer rainy season (it was known at that time as the Plazuela de la Ciénaga – literally 'the little swampy square'). An additional hazard was that the city was plunged into almost total darkness after sunset. People hung great lanterns or smaller lamps in their doorways, and the owners of commercial premises in particular were obliged to illuminate the street corners, where their shops usually stood. The first carriages began

to appear and created a stir in the streets of the town. They took the place of the horses and sedan chairs used by the rich, and introduced social distinctions into Havana society, which had been until then relatively equal. By the end of the seventeenth century horse-drawn carriages were widely used, creating a previously unimaginable volume of traffic. Other significant changes were not seen until the end of the eighteenth century. The few improvements of the seventeenth century are reflected in some of the buildings erected in the centre of the town.

Havana society was still composed of its traditional groups: Europeans, black slaves (and some freed ones) and a few of the Indians who had managed to survive (they had formed a community in the neighbouring village of Guanabacoa, as previously mentioned, and made ceramic wares there). Some of the Spanish families had acquired a certain social status and claimed descent from the first conquistadors. They built the most impressive houses of the period, although these were as yet far from being ostentatious displays of wealth. Over the years these houses were embellished with the architectural elements which were to become typical features of the traditional Creole house.

The function of patios and balconies

Houses were still built like fortresses, with thick walls, low-ceilinged rooms and few windows, but were gradually enlarged. The amount of living space and number of extensions grew to keep pace with increases in economic and social activities. In spite of this, the arrangement of space, with the rooms interconnecting on a rectangular plan, remained rigidly fixed. The inhabitants still lived in permanent fear of attack, and continued to plan their homes as a place of refuge. The compact, solidly built structures reflect their original protective and defensive function. The plain, symmetrical houses, with no openings on the outside, highlight both the limited technical and artistic skills of the builders at the time and the relatively modest means of the owners. The façade was a smoothly finished wall, throwing into relief the main entrance. This was unremarkable at first, but gradually became the most important decorative element of the façade, and one of the features most frequently used by the builders to display the wealth of the proprietors.

After the doorway, the most striking feature of the façade was a *cuarto esquinero* – a corner room on the upper floor similar to the *torres miradores* which are such a feature of Moorish architecture. The entrance to the house was usually at one end of the façade. It led into the *zaguán* or hall, a space which separated the doorway from the interior of the house, thus protecting the family's privacy.

Detail of the façade of No. 12 Calle Tacón in Havana.
There are still some traces of the original painted wall decorations.

The design of houses in Cuba has always had to take into account the often extreme weather conditions in this part of the Caribbean, where the intense heat of the sun alternates with torrential downpours. The patios and upper galleries, clearly influenced by the *mudéjar* style, were intended to deal with these local factors. They allowed for effective lighting and ventilation, and became such an integral part of domestic buildings that they are now the most distinctive feature of the Cuban colonial house.

Carved wooden details were typical of Cuban architecture of the seventeenth century. The woodwork of the balconies, balustrades and ceilings became progressively more intricate. Remarkable interlaced patterns were carved for the roof timbers, as well as other ornamentation characteristic of the Cuban baroque. Unfortunately, the over-use of the country's many varieties of trees led to their gradual extinction. Cedar, mahogany, white acacia and oaks had been abundant in the countryside and in gardens. They were used in house building, but also in much greater quantities to construct and repair ships in Havana's famous naval dockyards. Later on

Above: In the early colonial era houses in Havana were usually built facing the bay, like these in the old Calle Tacón, dating from the first half of the seventeenth century. These comparatively low-built houses have on the whole kept their original appearance. The taller block between the two low ones has an extra floor which was a later addition.

Above right: The *traspatio* or rear courtyard in the Casa de la Obra Pía in Havana. The floor of the gallery or loggia is of terracotta tiles. The various service rooms lead off it, including the kitchen (in the background, behind the arches) and the latrines.

Above: Detail of the wooden ceiling in the Casa de Diego Velázquez, on the corner of Calle Estrada Palma and Calle Aguilera in Santiago de Cuba. This finely carved ceiling is in the Spanish *mudéjar* style which predominated in Cuban architecture at the beginning of the colonial period.

Right: Detail of a door in the Casa de Diego Velázquez after restoration.

Opposite: The drawing-room of the Casa de Diego Velázquez after restoration. The oldest part of the house dates from the sixteenth century, but the whole building underwent various modifications during succeeding centuries. The restorers of the ceiling timbers used examples in other seventeenth-century Cuban houses as a guide in their work.

Above: 'Jalousies' or screens on the first-floor galleries in the Casa de Diego Velázquez.

Opposite: A room in the Casa de Diego Velázquez. During the restoration of the building this original window, with its strongly Moorish flavour, was uncovered and reconstructed, after its outline was noticed under the plaster.

wood was used as a fuel in the manufacture of sugar. Cuban hardwood was inevitably much employed from the beginning to build roofs with two or sometimes three pitches and straw was rapidly replaced with tiles. On the inside the structure of the roof was left exposed, and craftsmen began to carve the beams according to the style already familiar to them as people originally from southern Spain, where the Moorish style still dominated popular architecture. For this reason there are many old houses with *mudéjar*-style carved ceiling timbers. Some still visible today are good examples of the craftsmen's skill at combining their sources of inspiration creatively. These ceilings became an outstanding feature of the houses of the period.

It is also important to notice the widespread use of projecting eaves, which took different forms according to the particular period and the region of the country. Although highly decorative, they had an essentially functional role: they protected houses from violent rainstorms and reduced the impact of the sun by preventing it from shining directly on to the walls. The use of projecting eaves increased and they became notable ornamental features, particularly in provincial towns such as Trinidad.

The best surviving examples of houses from this period are in Havana. That on the corner of Calle Obrapía and Calle San Ignacio, the property of Don Gaspar Riberos de Vasconcelos, is especially notable and has a distinctive wooden balcony around the *cuarto esquinero*. The Casa de los Pimienta, No. 4 Calle Tacón, is also important, famous for its coffered ceilings. Although rebuilt in the eighteenth century, it has retained the character of the seventeenth, with the same reduced height, broad

Mudéjar-style screens enclosing the galleries
in the Casa de Diego Velázquez in Santiago
de Cuba. Other surviving screens in buildings
from the colonial era helped to ensure the
accuracy of the restoration, particularly the
wooden screens in the choir of the convent
of Santa Clara in Havana, which dates from
the seventeenth century.

proportions and general layout of the rooms. Unusually for the time, it has a mezzanine, but the house as a whole gives a good idea of how the richest families lived in the seventeenth century. The ground-floor rooms surrounding the patio were probably used by the house slaves, and to provide accommodation for the carriage and horses. The first floor has a balcony overlooking the bay and was used only by members of the family. Other typical features of the seventeenth-century style can also be seen on the nearby house, No. 12 Calle Tacón, notably its doorway – designed like many others to be the focus of attention, in spite of its simplicity. Following classical examples, these grand entrances are framed by pilasters and have a decorated entablature, highlighting the doorway on the otherwise plain walls of the façade.

The house on the corner of Calle Obrapía and Calle Mercaderes also has an impressive doorway. It is exceptional in Cuban architecture of the time for its scale and the style of its decoration. The layout of the rooms in this house (one of the most beautiful of its period) follows the usual pattern, in spite of later alterations. There is a patio surrounded on three sides by galleries, a *traspatio* (or rear courtyard) and many large rooms, several of which were added later. The impressive treatment of the internal spaces has made it one of the most interesting examples of Cuban colonial architecture. The original owner of the house funded religious good works in the capital, and his house as well as the street it stands in became known as 'Obrapía'.

Havana's most important families also lived in houses built on this palatial scale. One contemporary account describes their inhabitants: 'A multitude of birds with brilliant plumage emerged from these rustic nests. The men wore very brightly coloured clothes of French linen, silk and velvet. They had gold chains and rings, as well as swords and daggers, some of which were set with rich jewels. Compared with this, the effect made by the women seemed modest, even when dressed in all their finery.'[6]

The design for the typical Cuban house had reached its final form by the end of the eighteenth century, the result of the creative adaptation of styles from abroad to the local climate and materials. In the succeeding centuries its basic elements were built on and modified to suit changes in the customs and daily lives of the inhabitants.

Above: This house in old Havana on the corner of Calle Obrapía and Calle San Ignacio dates from the first half of the seventeenth century. The door is surmounted by the coat of arms of the original proprietor, Gaspar Riberos de Vasconcelos, captain and knight of the Order of Christ. It has certain architectural features inherited from the sixteenth century, such as the corner room. The wooden balcony on the corner of the two streets is original.

Opposite: Like all the seventeenth-century houses, No. 4 Calle Tacón in Havana has a patio running from front to rear of the site and galleries above. The plainness of the wooden balustrades and the columns supporting the corridors is in marked contrast with the highly decorated eighteenth-century balconies and galleries.

Opposite: Exposed structural woodwork is characteristic of Cuban architecture at the beginning of the colonial period. This example in the reception rooms of No. 4 Calle Tacón, Havana, is one of the finest to survive. Its magnificent design shows off the high degree of skill of the local craftsmen, who had completely assimilated the originally Spanish style. Note the moulded rafters supporting the pitched roof-sections and the highly ornamented central panel.

Right: On the top floor at No. 4 Calle Tacón the roof over the gallery is supported on wooden columns with small capitals. At this time the corridors were still very narrow. They allowed easier circulation within the house and helped to provide shelter from the sun. The tiled roof was sloped down towards the patio so that rainwater could be collected in cisterns or tubs.

Right: A detail from the doorway opposite.

Opposite: Doorway to the Casa de la Obra Pía in Havana. According to some experts, it was built and carved in Spain, but the architect Daniel Taboada, who was in charge of its restoration, believes it was made in Cuba using the local porous stone from Jaimanita. (It is shown here with a covering of whitewash.) We know, however, that the magnificent marble coat of arms surmounting it was brought from Spain.

Above: One of the many reception rooms in the Casa de la Obra Pía, Havana.

Opposite: Trefoil arch above the entrance to the private apartments in the Casa de la Obra Pía. When the house was rearranged and modernized at the end of the eighteenth century, a number of Baroque motifs, then in fashion in the capital, were added.

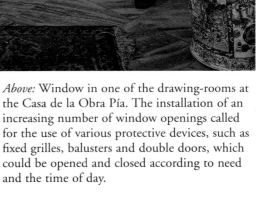

Previous pages: Patio of the Casa de la Obra Pía in Havana. In this seventeenth-century building the gallery runs around only three sides of the patio. In the following century, when the patio had definitively become the heart of the Cuban home, many of the original ones were rebuilt or enlarged.

Above: Window in one of the drawing-rooms at the Casa de la Obra Pía. The installation of an increasing number of window openings called for the use of various protective devices, such as fixed grilles, balusters and double doors, which could be opened and closed according to need and the time of day.

The Casa de la Obra Pía, with an area of more than a thousand square metres, contained the largest reception rooms in the city when it was built; one of them is shown above. The house is now the premises of a cultural institution.

Opposite: A fine example of Cuban Baroque: this multi-centred arch separates the sitting-room from the dining-room (which has a wooden penthouse roof) in the Casa del Dominicano in Trinidad.

Right: Houses in Trinidad were built with traditional tiled roofs of two or more pitches. They had wooden rafters, as in this house in Calle Amargura.

The power of the Creoles in the eighteenth century

The development of the colony

In the eighteenth century periods of unrest and insecurity gave way to an era of greater prosperity. General living standards, which had been rising for some time, continued to do so as housing quality improved. Stone-walled houses were more frequently built and gradually replaced the rustic *bohíos*. There was an increase in public and religious building projects, and in the construction of fine, stately residences by the Creoles, who were beginning to take full advantage of their position.

These changes did not, of course, happen overnight, and were not consistent throughout the country. The situation in the colony did not radically improve until after the British had seized Havana. In the first half of the eighteenth century conditions on the island remained relatively poor. Spain had been continuously in conflict with the other European maritime powers over the question of trade with the New World since the sixteenth century, and traders and adventurers of all kinds were still to be found in the Caribbean area. In the eighteenth century this permanently unstable situation deteriorated to such an extent that the navies of the different powers in the region ultimately found themselves fighting full-scale colonial wars. In 1762 the British army attacked Havana, and remained in control there for almost a year. A series of measures was introduced with the intention of giving the island a completely new commercial perspective. When Spain regained the colony a year later in exchange for Florida, the new rulers found that they could not go back to the old ways. Although partisan, the remarks by a British officer, a Major Joseph Gorham, on the social and material conditions in the country are interesting. He paints an admittedly unflattering picture of the Creoles, but it helps to give an idea of the situation in Havana at the time. 'The gentlemen's homes were mansions with at least ten or twelve rooms. These members of the highest society are courteous and affable, but apparently indolent, and love rich, loudly coloured clothes and furniture … .'[7]

The people of Cuba were beginning to be proud of their country and were no doubt irritated by the arrogance of the British, but they quickly understood the advantage of an approach to government that was less restrictive and centralized than that practised by the Spaniards. So Cuba embarked on a period of rapid change. The effect of this new freedom was soon apparent. With the foundations for a new beginning in place, the second half of the eighteenth century saw a series of social and economic developments and an increase in the construction of all kinds of civil and religious buildings.

Imposing residences were also built at that period for the representatives of the Spanish monarchy and for those families who had grown prosperous. In the eighteenth century there was already a patrician element in Cuba, particularly in Havana, which did much to destroy the old concept of an egalitarian society. Some of these new aristocrats had been claiming descent from the conquistadors since the previous century, and often acquired noble titles taken from the names of newly established villages. This happened for instance at Jaruco and Santa María del Rosario, whose founders derived various titles from the names in the neighbourhood. A number of families in the élite of eighteenth-century Cuban society were keen to have certain exclusive powers and the creation of an aristocracy with officially recognized coats of arms helped them to achieve their aim. This development affected the whole community, as the accumulation of wealth accentuated social differences. The crucially important defence of the city, which until now had been the concern of all the inhabitants, was soon a responsibility assumed by only a small number of them. In this way the strong bonds which had previously united Havana's citzens began to be loosened.

Alongside this aristocracy a middle class began to establish itself, consisting of a rather less wealthy group drawn from the ranks of the liberal professions, the Church, the military and government officials. The extraordinary commercial development which took place after 1760 also resulted in the creation of a business class on the fringes of the aristocracy, consisting mostly of new arrivals, whose status improved in the following century. The poor whites were for the most part clerks, shop assistants and sailors.

Opposite: The dilapidated state of these walls reveals the materials used in many of the houses in Trinidad. It was a brick-making area, and brick was used to build the *ingenios* or sugar mills, as well as some individual houses like this one.

The arrival of large numbers of slaves to work in the sugar industry, which had grown rapidly since the British opened up the market, involved the imposition of certain codes of behaviour throughout society, and people's day-to-day lives changed. From now on there were established differences of colour, race, income and authority. The population of the towns rapidly split into separate white, black and mixed-race groups. Not only blacks and whites but also slaves and free men lived very differently. The poor whites and the rich property owners (and the ruling élite in general) now lived in separate worlds. However, the most glaring difference was the one which opened up between strangers and *naturales* or 'natives', that is, between the Spaniards who had only recently arrived and the Creoles born on the island. From the eighteenth century onwards the question of being a *natural* became so important that it was also a factor in the lives of the children of slaves – the blacks having just come from Africa being treated differently from those born in Cuba. Housing reflected these social distinctions, which became more and more marked. This was particularly noticeable in Havana, where the traditional dwellings of wood and palm leaves, originally forming the inner core of the city, now disappeared from the centre and were concentrated on the outskirts, near the ramparts. At the same time there was a substantial increase in stone-built houses with tiled roofs within the city walls. The modest seventeenth-century houses were in the process of being transformed into much bigger and more luxurious residences. By the end of the century some of the stone houses inhabited by the ruling élite were of an exceptional quality.

Opposite: This loggia in the Beltrán de Santa Cruz family home was enclosed in the nineteenth century. One of the members of the family was given the title of Conde de Jaruco. The famous María de las Mercedes Santa Cruz y Montalvo, Condesa de Merlín, played in this room as a child. The design and colours of the glass panels filling the large arches make it one of the most handsome rooms of the period.

Right: A window looking on to the street in a house in Calle Amargura, Trinidad.

Overleaf: Calle San José, Trinidad. The projecting windows with their wooden grilles are built on to a stone window seat. People inside can use it as a vantage point to observe what is happening in the street.

The Creole house opens on to the street

Broadly speaking, all the houses built at this time retained the traditional horizontal layout. They still had thick walls, and the functional aspects of the buildings were more important than their decoration. The various architectural elements reflected an underlying continuity in the evolution of Cuban houses. It must be remembered that they had always been designed to take account of the climate, particularly the intense heat which affected the island nearly all the year round. For this reason attention was focused on building roofs using materials and techniques which would provide some kind of insulation. High roofs had proved to be an effective way of diminishing the heat, and the principle was extended during the eighteenth century to the use of much taller pillars in the construction of the buildings. This allowed the air to circulate more freely and

59

keep the inside of the houses cool, and the increased height of the structural elements became a typical Cuban feature. Later on, the high ceilings were not only regarded as a practical necessity, but additionally their elaborate carving came to symbolize the wealth and sumptuous lifestyle of the owners.

Another way of improving the ventilation, so necessary in this hot climate, was to create more openings in the walls (as far as was technically possible at the time). Doors and windows, which were usually of similar proportions, began to increase in number and size. The new spatial organization thus created allowed greater freedom of movement within the house. Intercommunicating rooms permitted increased ventilation, which was more important than privacy in the daily lives of the family. Windows were eventually built to the full height of the walls, and were distinguished from the external doors by a different decorative treatment. Although these numerous large windows resolved the important question of ventilation, they raised other difficulties. Ways had to be found, for instance, to control the amount of strong sunlight coming through such a large number of openings, as well as the water that penetrated during the frequent heavy downpours at certain seasons. This was resolved by fitting the arcades of the internal galleries and the fanlights of the doors and windows with shutters and *lucetas* (coloured glass panels) which kept out both the light and the torrential rain. The early *lucetas* developed into the spectacular coloured windows to be found in increasing numbers in the grand houses, particularly in Havana, and became one of the great traditions of the Cuban colonial house. However, in a few places (Trinidad, for example) these features were almost unknown, and screens made with strips of wood or louvres were used instead to serve the same purpose.

The main doorway remained the central feature of the façade and the focus of new decorative styles. The doors themselves, and the door frames, were built on a new, larger scale. They had to be big enough to permit the passage of the horse-drawn carriages (usually kept within the building) that were used by the families to travel about the town. It must be borne in mind that Cuban ladies stayed in their carriages and never set foot in the street – hence the importance of increasing the size of the main door to let the carriages pass through. However, it was also necessary to allow access for the loading and unloading of goods on the ground floor. Obviously it was impractical for such a huge doorway to remain permanently open. Sometimes, therefore, much smaller doors were built beside the carriage entrance, or cut out of the main doors, to facilitate the comings and goings of the family, servants and visitors.

Above: The Casa del Dominicano was built in Trinidad towards the end of the eighteenth century. Because of the uneven terrain, it has an external flight of steps, or perron, at the front of the building as well as one at the side and a narrow front gallery. The shape of the windows and their projecting grilles, the undulating mouldings and wooden balusters are unusual. This façade is one of the finest examples of Cuban Baroque architecture.

Opposite: The monumental doorway of the Palacio Pedroso, No. 64 Calle de Cuba, in Havana. The studded wooden door has the traditional smaller wicket openings cut into it. As was usual before the eighteenth century the façade is without an arcade and the doors and windows open directly on to the road. The mezzanine windows have individual balconies. On the first floor a balcony with columns, a canopy and turned wooden balusters runs the whole length of the façade.

Opposite: Detail of the wall of an eighteenth-century house in Trinidad, where a window has been converted into a door.

Below right: Archway in the second vestibule of the Casa del Conde de Casa Lombillo in Havana. It links the small patio from the original building with the new entrance at one end of the arcade. The beautiful grille was installed in the twentieth century and comes from a demolished nineteenth-century building. It shows Cuban ironwork at the peak of its achievement.

The individual elements of these imposing doorways, all ornamented in their own way, created a handsome ensemble. The doors themselves were built of precious woods with carefully chosen fittings: the studs, knockers and other details were made of wrought iron with a great variety of decorative motifs. Each doorway now also had cast-iron guards to protect the stone bases from damage by the carriage wheels. These features were answers to practical problems, but were also intended to enhance the pleasing effect of the whole building, making it stand out from the others around it.

For a large part of the eighteenth century the purpose of the *zaguán,* like its counterpart in Moorish architecture, was to protect the inhabitants from curious eyes and to preserve their privacy. It separated the door from the patio and functioned as a vestibule. When this space began to be used to house the carriage, it became necessary for it to be enlarged. It had to be made even bigger if a staircase was added, taking up space on one side. The area was now given a certain dignity by building graceful arches to separate it from the patio.

The houses built by the settlers had always faced inwards in order to protect the residents from attack by strangers, which was then very common in the towns. As a result the outside appearance of the houses was almost entirely blank.

Previous pages and above: Staircase at the rear of the patio in the Casa del Conde de Bayona in Havana. The original entrance was in the Calle San Ignacio. When the building was altered the staircase was retained, which explains its unusual position for the period. The whole of the ground floor is paved with stone from San Miguel – an appropriate surface for the original commercial use of the building at street level.

Opposite: View from the main entrance to the building. The foreground area is the vestibule. Behind it is the arcade which gives on to the patio. At the back is the double flight of stairs which leads up to the private apartments. Today this building houses the Museum of Colonial Art.

Opposite: Mezzanine floors were increasingly built in Cuban houses to make space for a larger number of offices and to accommodate more servants and employees. The finest example is this one in the Palacio de los Capitanes Generales in Havana, which used to house the offices of the colonial administration and the prison.

Right: Detail of the Museum of Education in the Plaza de la Catedral in Havana. Arcades are the most significant innovation made in the eighteenth century to the architecture of the street façade. They mirror the colonnades around the central patio in traditional buildings plans.

Inside, however, the rooms opened on to the patio – a throwback to the Arab customs of southern Spain, the original home of many of the inhabitants. The whole space centred on the patio which in time became the focal point of the house and the principal source of light and ventilation. Plants, water pitchers and pots of flowers were collected around the fountains and their basins, adding to the attractive and welcoming atmosphere. Beyond the patio was a *traspatio,* or back yard, which was used for a number of domestic tasks. It must be pointed out that at this time neither the kitchen nor the washrooms were part of the main house, and were reached from the back yard.

The internal colonnades, which protected the house from the heat and the frequent summer downpours, were enlarged to improve circulation between the rooms. On the first floor some houses had wooden projecting galleries dating from the seventeenth century, built to improve access to the various parts of the house. These, too, underwent modification. The narrow first-floor corridors were originally balconies with tiled roofs, supported by little columns and wooden balustrades (sometimes the date of construction of the building can be deduced from their decorative details). Eventually these balconies were linked up and ran right round the patio, becoming more like the much bigger colonnades to be seen in the most luxurious residences of the eighteenth century.

The ground-floor colonnades supporting the upper galleries were to play a crucial role in these buildings, and became one of the principal elements in the relationship between the internal spaces. When these arcades were added on the street side of the building, they became part of the urban landscape and changed the general appearance of the city. They made a particular impact on the main squares during the eighteenth century. The supporting columns have a distinctive style, reflecting the fertile imagination and exuberance displayed by the stonemasons at different periods.

Little balconies appeared at the outside first-floor windows, as we have seen, creating a closer relationship with the street. In the eighteenth century these individual balconies were joined to form a continuous one along the whole façade. They became indispensable to the social lives of families who, far from wanting to hide themselves, were now keen to establish the dialogue between inside and outside that was to become so characteristic of the Cuban house. The wooden balconies – later also made of iron –

71

quickly became an integral part of the façades. The way they were built and the detailed decoration of the balustrades naturally depended on the skill of the builders and the stylistic influences at the time.

During the eighteenth century woodworking skills reached their highest technical and artistic levels, as can be seen in most of the examples that remain today. Nevertheless, during the last years of the century there was a tendency to replace wood with iron for some of the architectural details. Some rooms in the houses of the period had decorative dados painted in bright colours, usually with floral and geometric motifs.

External influences were readily assimilated, taking into account the demands of the climate, and this led to the development of types of buildings which successfully combined practicality with style. Certain elements would define the eighteenth-century Cuban colonial house: tall pillars, internal patios, galleries, arcades and columns. Some formal details were borrowed from the Spanish Baroque (which had flourished in Spain during the previous century), but according to some contemporary commentators the Cuban people also responded to something which they found particularly congenial in the whole spirit of the Baroque style. Refinements in domestic life became linked with a parallel tendency towards exuberance, which perhaps explains the both functional and ornamental character of Cuban houses. Those architectural details inherited from the Spanish Baroque are the doorways, arches, columns and, above all, the balconies with their undulating balusters, which today recall one of the most creative periods of colonial architecture.

Opposite: This house on the corner of Calle Mercaderes and Calle Amargura in old Havana was built by Don Francisco Basabe at the beginning of the eighteenth century. The balcony columns are of turned wood; the wrought-iron balustrade was added in the following century.

Trade and the growth of Havana

The growth of Havana was gradual at the beginning of the century, but certain changes that took place after 1730 brought about a rapid increase in the building of private houses. Most of these were to be found in the streets adjoining the Plaza de Armas, which was the focus of the colonial administration. Among these streets were Calle Obrapía, Calle Mercaderes, Calle Oficios and Calle Lamparilla, which eventually became some of main thoroughfares of the city.

On the whole, new roads were laid out in accordance with old Havana's original grid-like plan. They ran in parallel lines towards the east and the Plaza Nueva (today the Plaza Vieja), where some of the grandest houses of the colonial period were built. The streets were often named after the trades represented there. Calle Mercaderes, for instance, was the site of a large number of merchants' shops and warehouses. These establishments were open nearly all day, selling goods from overseas brought by the Spanish fleet and by other ships which put into the port. Another street, Calle Oficios, was so called because it was lined with offices and workshops.

Above and opposite: The patio of No. 16 Calle Oficios in the old part of Havana. The house was built between the end of the eighteenth century and the beginning of the nineteenth. The use of space is typical of the period. The dining-room on the first floor is situated in the loggia between the patio and the rear patio to ensure maximum ventilation. It can be closed off with wooden shutters and has large decorative glass panes, very common in the nineteenth century. Today it is used by a cultural institution, the Casa de los Arabes.

The buildings in the Plaza de la Catedral form one of the most magnificent eighteenth-century townscapes. The Plaza is the busiest and best-known of Havana's squares, with some fine early eighteenth-century private houses. On the left is the Casa del Marqués de Aguas Claras, built in 1720 (it is now the El Patio restaurant). The cathedral has a particularly Cuban Baroque façade and is one of the island's most famous sights.

The rudimentary lighting system for public places that had been installed in the seventeenth century was no longer adequate for a town which now numbered more than 25,000 inhabitants, and was beginning to have a significant amount of traffic in the streets after dark. Everything was organized according to the hours of sunlight; people were on the move at daybreak. At the end of the afternoon, between six and seven o'clock, the church bells called them to prayer. After that, there were only two hours left for the evening walk before it became dark. Places of public entertainment did not exist (apart from the taverns and inns, often of ill repute), and people had to make do with official celebrations and those organized from time to time by the Church. Towards the end of the century the residents of Havana, who had previously hardly ventured beyond the city walls, began to go out to enjoy the coastal scenery and the surrounding countryside. Of course, such outings were largely limited to families possessing their own carriage and horses.

The rather uncomfortable carriages of the previous century had been replaced by barouches – two-wheeled, horse-drawn carriages with a leather hood which could be folded down in good weather. They were made more comfortable by the leather webbing which acted as a shock absorber. A *calesero* or coachman always drove, carrying up to three passengers. Most of those who could afford to had a carriage of their own, but relatively few had houses with enough space to store them. They were obliged to put the carriage in their biggest room, next to the entrance, as if it were an extra-large piece of furniture.

Records show that residents of Havana were well dressed, but that their clothes were simpler than those worn in Spain, everyone dressing according to their means. Normally, the richest families obtained their clothes from the Iberian peninsula.

The houses of the merchants of Havana

The increased productivity of the rural areas and the expansion of foreign trade meant that a great variety of goods arrived in the capital, where they were stored in warehouses before being transported by ship. In this way Havana was both a storehouse and a port for all the produce of the region, and became rich on the proceeds. To accommodate the increasing scale of commercial operations larger warehouses were needed. Similarly, houses needed to be bigger as they became used for an increasing number of activities. Throughout the century the houses of Havana's ruling élite underwent a series of changes which considerably affected their overall appearance. Two-storey dwellings with a mezzanine became common, and ground-floor arcades were added to the street façades for the greater convenience of pedestrians.

Opposite: Arcaded façade of a house looking on to the Plaza de la Catedral, Havana.

Right: View of the cathedral from the drawing-room of the Casa del Conde de Bayona, built in 1720 by Don Luis Chacón, governor of Cuba. The doors, wooden shutters and coloured window panes above the opening were designed to regulate the amount of air and light coming into the house. The house's prominent position opposite the cathedral allowed its residents a perfect view of events in the square.

The middle classes were also building. Their houses were single-storey and had no entrance hall or carriage store. Built in far larger numbers than the grand houses, they made a bigger impact on the general appearance of the town. In both larger and smaller houses the ground floor increased in size and was used in a more practical way. The internal patios were bigger, and their fountains were now able to supply all the water needed by the household, avoiding reliance on the public distribution of water of inferior quality.

In the early days, domestic and commercial functions had been able to coexist within the houses. But as the demands of daily life became more complex, the situation became increasingly uncomfortable. The richest families resorted to building another floor for their own use, taking refuge there from the intense activity below. The mezzanine and annexes were left to the household's slaves. Once these separate spaces had been established and allocated, the Creole house assumed its definitive form in the residences of the aristocracy. The ground

The Casa del Conde de Bayona is the only house in the Plaza de la Catedral that still retains its seventeenth-century façade. The son-in-law of the first owner, Don José Bayona y Chacón, made some important changes in the early eighteenth century but, unlike the owners of neighbouring houses, he never built an arcade facing the square.

Right and opposite: Reception rooms in the Casa del Conde de Bayona. As can be seen, these rooms are particularly spacious. During the nineteenth century rocking chairs became indispensable to the Cuban way of life, and are still found in some private houses. The collectors' items displayed in the cabinet – Spanish and French fans, opaline vases and bibelots – and the Baccarat crystal chandeliers hanging from the wooden ceiling are examples of the great variety of decorative objects imported from Europe by aristocratic families in the nineteenth century.

floor was reserved for warehousing, the carriage and the annexes. The intermediate level was for the servants and the kitchens, and above that the family had a whole floor to itself. This arrangement was established by the end of the eighteenth century, but became the norm only in the nineteenth, when an increasing number of families had the means to build their own homes. Before that the most widespread change was in the number and size of the rooms on the ground floor, according to the pattern established in the seventeenth century. In Havana the best examples of houses dating from the eighteenth century are to be found in the three most important squares: the Plaza de Armas, the Plaza de la Catedral and the Plaza Vieja. The busiest and most famous square in the capital has always been the Plaza de la Catedral (or Santa Iglesia), very close to the sea front. Some of the most beautiful houses of the period were built near the Cathedral, whose façade is a fine example of the Cuban Baroque.

Above: Arcade along the façades of the Casa del Marqués de Arcos and the Casa del Conde de Casa Lombillo on one side of the Plaza de la Catedral in Havana.

Opposite: The Casa del Marqués de Arcos was built in 1741. When Diego Peñalver, the Treasurer of Royal Finances, became the owner of this house he added an extra floor and built the arcade.

Opposite the Cathedral is the Casa del Conde de Bayona (not the original owner). The façade facing the square is typical of the houses built at the beginning of the eighteenth century. The neighbouring houses (those of the Marqués de Arcos, the Conde de la Casa Lombillo and the Marqués de Aguas Claras) were transformed by adding covered arcades – a practice which increased at the end of the century, as we have seen. Near the square is another particularly beautiful eighteenth-century house, the Casa del Conde de la Reunión. The writer Alejo Carpentier used it in his novel *El Siglo de las Luces* as the setting for the story of his main characters. The patio with its narrow galleries on three sides and the wonderful carving of the wooden balustrades, doorways and windows have made this house one of the most famous examples of the Cuban Baroque. The Plaza Vieja was for a long time the site of one of the main markets, where people came to buy their daily provisions and other goods. It was also the place where men (including the emancipated blacks) went to have their hair cut.

The large houses in the square were all residences of the Creole aristocracy. Some of them have been restored and are now used by various cultural institutions. The Casa del Conde San Juan de Jaruco (currently the Cuban Cultural Heritage Fund) retains certain characteristic features of eighteenth-century homes. The coloured glass windows are among the most beautiful examples in colonial Cuban architecture. There are also some fine wall paintings in the first-floor rooms and around the staircase leading to the upper floor. The Casa de las Hermanas Cárdenas, also situated in the Plaza Vieja, is an equally typical eighteenth-century house. Its internal patio with galleries on two sides and its pleasant terrace were valuable amenities for the original occupants.

The sumptuous residences of the most senior representatives of the monarchy (those of the Capitán General and the Segundo Cabo), built at the end of the eighteenth century,

The Casa del Conde de la Reunión in Havana was built on a long narrow plot hardly ten metres wide and was eventually enlarged at the rear. The wood carving (doors, balustrades and ceiling mouldings) and the mural paintings are very decorative, displaying the skills of local craftsmen. The wrought-iron grille was added in the nineteenth century.

87

Left: The Casa del Conde de la Reunión, No. 215 Calle Empedrado, in old Havana. Its first owner, Santiago de la Cuesta, later given the title of Conde de la Reunión de Cuba, was one of the island's first slave traders. The façade of this house is typical of eighteenth-century dwellings that were built in narrow streets and therefore had no room for an arcade. Notable features are the wooden shutters, the glass window panels, the turned wood of the balustrades, the grilles and the small balconies.

Opposite: Patio of the Casa del Conde de la Reunión, where the owner had his business premises. The ground floor was used as storage space for goods and the mezzanine was used by the employees. The doors and balconies look on to the patio. Although small, it is one of the most charming examples of Cuban colonial architecture.

Opposite: The inside of the Casa del Conde de la Reunión seen from the main entrance. The handsome multi-centred arch – a frequent motif in Cuban eighteenth-century Baroque buildings – defines the entrance and the position of the staircase leading to the private upper floor. Today this house is the headquarters of the Fundación Alejo Carpentier – the Cuban author used it as the setting for his novel *El Siglo de las Luces.*

Above: The studded wooden main door and the stone flags are original. The use of glazed tiles to decorate dados and to protect the lower parts of the ground-floor walls from damp became common practice during the nineteenth century.

encapsulate all the features of colonial domestic architecture. At the time they were distinguished by their size and magnificence, and came to be representative of the colonial power in Havana. Some of the architectural details were copied in the new houses built within the city walls. These included the patios, arcades and columns, of which these two houses have some of the finest examples, but other details, often regarded as of lesser interest (such as, for example, the decoration of the doors and windows – the *jamba habanera*), are considered by some historians to be equally important to the Havana style of the time.

Housing in the provincial areas

Although private houses in Havana had achieved the degree of sophistication already described, the wood and palm-leaf *bohíos* inherited from the original inhabitants were still the standard dwelling for the peasants in the rural areas. They were also to be found in the provincial capitals, and on the outskirts of Havana itself, where the poorest people

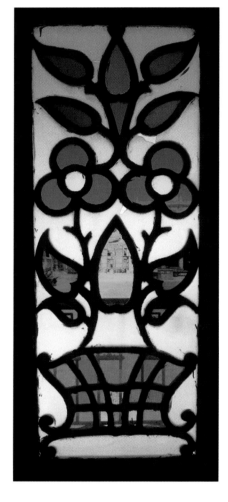

lived. However, in the country regions the richest families continued to live in relative simplicity, even in the larger towns.

The more durable building materials were not yet available in the Cuban countryside and did not come into general use there until the end of the eighteenth century and the beginning of the nineteenth, when the living conditions of the landowners had become considerably more settled.

In the eighteenth century the peasants (who hardly had a social life) were clad in cheap, light cotton clothes suitable for the climate. They often wore long wide trousers with loose shirts (the traditional *guayabera*). Only the more prosperous peasants had leather shoes. Wide-brimmed felt hats were gradually replaced with ones made of woven *yarey* leaves, which were cheaper and more suitable for the hot climate.

There are, unfortunately, few examples left of houses dating from the sixteenth, seventeenth or eighteenth centuries in the provincial towns of Cuba. The frequent hurricanes, earth tremors (mostly concentrated in eastern areas), even the occasional armed conflict

Previous pages: The Plaza Vieja in Havana was the site of the city's main market during the colonial period. Around it are some important eighteenth-century houses built for the Creole aristocracy. Spacious stone arcades line the façades. Some of the upstairs loggias have been enclosed to increase the size of reception rooms.

Left: Window in the Casa del Conde San Juan de Jaruco. Side and upper panels of doors and windows were sometimes filled in with decorative glass.

Opposite: Patio of the Casa del Conde San Juan de Jaruco. The practice of including the ground floor and the mezzanine in a single arcade meant that the upper galleries of eighteenth-century houses were also built on a more generous scale.

Opposite: Patio and galleries of the Palacio de los Capitanes Generales, Plaza de Armas, Havana. The use of stone balustrades on the roof line was frequent in the nineteenth century, coinciding with the replacement of pitched, wooden-tile-covered roofs with flat terraced ones.

Right: Casa del Conde San Juan de Jaruco in Havana: arch at the foot of the stairs leading up to the private apartments.

Left: A gallery window in the Palacio del Segundo Cabo in Havana with decorated glass pane and wooden shutters. This alternative way of closing windows was introduced in the nineteenth century and improved ventilation.

Above: Stone staircase in the Casa de las Hermanas Cárdenas, in Havana's Plaza Vieja. As in other eighteenth-century buildings, an extra flight of stairs had to be added to allow for the combined height of the ground floor and the mezzanine.

Opposite: Second-floor corridor in the Palacio del Segundo Cabo, Havana.

which sometimes erupted between country towns and of course the poor durability of the building materials used were all factors in the disappearance of a large number of buildings. Those which did survive clearly show that they did not reach the standard of the ones built in Havana. However, some in Santiago de Cuba, Camagüey and Trinidad still have certain features characteristic of the period. In Santiago, for instance, the houses had to be built taking into account the irregularity of the terrain. They were constructed on raised plinths and provided with steps up from the road. Houses in Camagüey were known for their distinctive multi-lobed archways. The very large earthenware jars that householders used to keep in their patios also gave a very individual character to the houses of the region. Some of the houses in Trinidad are reminders of the town's increasing importance during the eighteenth century (although it was not at the height of its prosperity until a hundred years later). They have some beautifully crafted woodwork and eaves boards which set them apart from others of the same period.

The houses built during the eighteenth century in these unassuming provincial towns were of a single storey at street level and had no *zaguán*. The dwellings of even the most prosperous families in these regions were more like those of the middle classes in the capital.

Left: One of the large reception rooms and (*below*) the dining room in the Palacio de los Capitanes Generales in Havana, with a reconstruction of the original decor as part of the City Museum which now occupies the building. The wood and stone used are local, but many of the materials (Italian marble for the floors and stairs, Spanish metalwork) and decorative objects, like those on display here, were imported from Europe. The mansion was built between 1776 and 1791 and first occupied by the island's governor, Don Luis de Las Casas.

Opposite: Patio of the Palacio de los Capitanes Generales. The Baroque motifs in the spandrels were subsequently copied in many other buildings in Havana and in other Cuban towns. No contemporary building had a patio erected on such a scale, with such a noble stone arcade around it. A statue of Christopher Columbus stands in the middle. It was made in Italy and brought to Havana in the second half of the nineteenth century.

Opposite: Wooden shutters became widely used during the nineteenth century, particularly to enclose the arcades on the first floor. Those in the Palacio del Segundo Cabo in Calle O'Reilly have a combination of shutters and coloured glass fanlights.

Above: Grille in the archway to the vestibule in the Palacio del Segundo Cabo. It was added in the nineteenth century, when Cuban architecture was dominated by the art of wrought-iron decoration. This mansion was built between 1772 and 1791 and was originally used for various administrative purposes by the officials of the Spanish monarchy.

Detail of the façade of a house at the corner
of Calle Santa Ana and Calle Media Luna in
Trinidad. The curved window with turned
balusters is unusual. An elderly woman is always
sitting behind the balusters ready to talk.

Façade of an eighteenth-century house in Trinidad. The Spanish-style doorway, decorated with metal studs, has a half-door of local design cut into it. The windows can be closed in two ways – with a grille or with half shutters. The shutters would be used on very windy days, and during heatwaves only the grilles protected the inside of the houses.

105

Opposite: The house at No. 261 Calle de Santa Rita in Santiago. With its projecting balcony, turned wooden balustrade and tiled roof supported on square posts, it resembles some of the oldest houses in Havana.

Above: The use of roofs with more than one pitch led to the appearance of various kinds of eaves to shade the walls. They lend a distinctive character to Cuban towns, as can be seen in this view of Calle Media Luna in Trinidad.

Above: This house, No. 236 Calle Gloria in Trinidad, is thought to be one of the oldest in the town, dating from the end of the seventeenth century or the beginning of the eighteenth. With its stone walls and symmetrically pitched roof, it follows the traditional design of corner houses in Havana. Here, too, the ground floor was intended for trade and the upper floor for living space. It has no roofed balcony and recalls the old, plainer houses with *mirador* corner rooms, which were built in the capital in the seventeenth century.

Opposite: Balcony of a house on the corner of Calle Cristo and Calle Rosario in Trinidad. It dates from the end of the seventeenth century.

Opposite: An unusual example of a door and window with matching decoration at Baracoa. This town at the eastern tip of the island had regular contact with neighbouring Caribbean islands and may have imported woodwork of this kind.

Right: Entrance to the Palacio Aldama in Havana within the street arcade. (This part of the building was originally the residence of Rosa and Domingo del Monte.) The architrave to the traditional wooden door is very simple, compared with the Baroque ornamentation of earlier buildings. The door is set off instead by two large street-lamps and the oculus above the entrance. Wrought iron is an important decorative element in this building.

The Spanish colony in the nineteenth century

Growth and recession

New opportunities opened up for Cuba at the end of the eighteenth century and in the early years of the nineteenth, at a time of great political change in Europe. The era in which Cuba's importance depended solely on its strategic position was over, and the island began to be appreciated on its own terms and for its own resources. Havana was no longer just a port of call, but had become the highly developed centre of Cuba's export trade. Great fortunes had been made from the growth of industry and commerce – the expansion of the *ingenios* (sugar plantations and mills) and *cafetales* [8] (coffee plantations) – as well as from the first foreign investments. Other parts of the country benefited from these favourable conditions, some towns experiencing an economic growth previously unknown outside the capital. Increased production and exports required, amongst other things, financial resources beyond the scope of individual owners. As a result banks, businesses and limited companies (both Spanish and Creole) were set up, laying the foundations for the financial activity (sometimes speculative) which was to intensify in the years to come. By 1820 huge fortunes had already been amassed from sugar production. Don Domingo de Aldama, for example, had made enough money to be entirely self-financing. Many other families increased their already large fortunes through the sugar trade. Other important figures in Cuba's economic expansion, such as Don Joaquín Gómez and the Conde de Santovenia, also made a notable contribution to the history of Cuban architecture with the houses they built for their own use.

The prosperity enjoyed on the island during the first half of the nineteenth century was to make Cuba famous. Visitors of various nationalities have left accounts of this new affluence after visiting the island's largest towns. On arriving in Havana in 1839 the Spaniard José Jacinto Salas y Quiroga described his 'pride in this leading Spanish port, so large and prosperous, so full of people and activity, with so many ships, flags, and smaller boats, and such a mixture of voices, cargoes and workers on the wide and well-organized landing stages. It is possible for large three-masted ships to tie up there, so that more than one hundred of them at a time can easily be loaded and unloaded directly from the shore. This constant noise, this busy, animated scene is a source of pride and joy, though a traveller arriving here from the now abandoned and wasted port of Cadiz also feels a certain sadness.'[9]

The expansive conditions prevailing in the first few decades of the nineteenth century were favourable to new public and industrial building projects throughout the island. During these years the colony was at the peak of its prosperity. It was at this time that theatres were built in the country's larger towns. They form an important part of the history of Cuban architecture, and fortunately many of them have been restored so that we are now able to see them in all their original magnificence.

A simple house at Baracoa, typical of those in provincial towns. It is made of wood, with a tiled roof, and has no other decoration than the coloured paint on the wooden planks of the walls.

Another positive development was the growth of tile- and brick-making works, the bricks being used to build the *ingenios* and *cafetales*. Two important events had a crucial impact on the towns, and above all on the capital. The first School of Master Builders, Surveyors and Quantity Surveyors (Escuela de Maestros de Obras, Agrimensores y Apare-jadores) was founded in Havana in 1851, and building regulations were laid down for Havana and the surrounding villages in 1861.

The colony's economic expansion was vast in the first decades, but subsequent recessions in the second half of the nineteenth century caused a long period of instability, characterized by a deterioration in living standards and a relentless struggle for independence on the part of the Cubans. Under these conditions building projects were reduced to a minimum, and many of the towns failed to prosper. Buildings were often converted to other uses, which led to the loss of important examples of local architecture. Such losses had other causes, too. Some towns and villages, mostly in the southern areas, suffered as a result of conflicts between them (Camagüey and part of Las Villas were badly affected). In spite of all this, towns such as Havana, Matanzas, Cárdenas and Cienfuegos enjoyed relative stability, allowing building work to continue, though at a slower pace than before.

The nineteenth century was a decisive one for Cuba. Some exceptional people made their mark, and not only in the political and military sphere. Scientists, writers and artists all contributed to the founding of a Cuban culture and identity. The Cuban people began

Opposite: The Governor's
Palace and (*above right*) the
Palacio Ferrer at Cienfuegos.

to articulate their dissatisfaction with the colonial government's ruthless exploitation of the country's resources and its total disregard for the most elementary rights of the rest of the community. Most of the population was concentrated at the prosperous western end of the island, and those born in Cuba now outnumbered the immigrants from Spain. It is hardly surprising that the war of independence began in the eastern part of the country, which was still marginalized and impoverished, in spite of the presence of a few wealthy Creole families descended from the original settlers. Although the island enjoyed a period of prosperity under the colonial regime at the beginning of the nineteenth century, deep antagonisms had sprung up between the Creoles and the Spanish monarchy. This showed itself in a variety of ways in the social, political and cultural life of the country. At the end of the 1850s the Creole bourgeoisie, now more numerous and better organized than at the beginning of the century, insisted that Spain concede the economic freedoms and political rights that would fit their country for the modern world. These demands were rejected by Spain which was intent on reinforcing its hold on Cuba after losing its other American colonies. This situation led inevitably to the outbreak of the Cuban war of independence at Bayamo on 10 October 1868. The first *mambises* or rebels began their campaign for their nation's freedom in the east of the country. Apart from a few intervals of peace, the struggle continued for most of the last three decades of the century. Many highly respected individuals supported Cuba's fight for independence, and were against all forms of colonial rule. The United States intervened in the war between Spain and Cuba and the American army remained on the island until the ratification of the new Republic of Cuba's constitution (including the Platt Amendment imposed by the United States government) and the election of the first president in 1902.

A multiracial population

During the nineteenth century the population of the country consisted of the Europeans and their Creole descendants (that is, those born on the island), who were both white and mixed-race, legitimate and illegitimate, and the blacks, either born on the island or brought over from Africa. Most of the Europeans were Spaniards, but there were also many French, German and English people, as well as a few from the United States and Latin America. The way of life and customs of these mostly European immigrants were gradually integrated into the Cuban traditions and contributed to the enrichment of the national culture. A German, Juan Tessel, is said to have opened the first copper mines in Cuba. A British company later took them over, and helped to develop the town of El Cobre in the mining area.

The growing importance of coffee as a commodity was the result of French immigration from Haiti. Coffee had previously been regarded as a curiosity in Cuba, but its cultivation soon became as vital to the colony's economy as the sugar-cane crop. The sophisticated lifestyle of the coffee plantation owners was distinctly French. Their cuisine, wines and fashions (very popular with the wealthiest ladies) gave them a certain kudos. The best restaurant in Havana in about 1860 was at No. 72 Calle Cuba (between Calle Obispo and Calle Obrapía), and was run by a Frenchman called François Garçon. He enjoyed a high reputation for his cooking, as well as for the wines that he imported from France and served with the meals. In fact, wine was increasingly in demand as the nineteenth century progressed. Contemporary newspaper accounts claim that the best shoemakers and finest dressmakers in the capital were all French.

The American influence was not limited to the businessmen who came to negotiate with Cuban merchants and industrialists. The island's climate attracted American tourists and it became one of their favourite destinations. They could escape the cold weather or enjoy a course of treatment at the thermal baths (their recuperative properties were famous in the nineteenth century). European travellers often commented on the American influence in Cuba in records of their travels: '… as soon as the month of November has begun the steam boats from New Orleans and liners from New York disgorge floods of passengers into the capital of the Spanish island … . It is interesting to see how much they enjoy being here, taking pleasure in the lovely countryside, or the Italian music which is much more widely heard here than in New York … .'[10]

Other authors, too, have made observations about the American influence on Cuban society. 'Civilization in Havana and in Cuba in general is a mixture imported from its neighbour, and it is precisely this mixture that is most surprising – the contrast between the Spanish civilization which is gradually disappearing and the modern American civilization which is gradually pervading Cuban life … . Everything about Havana, the surrounding villages, the inhabitants, their customs, their clothes, the very walls of the city have this ambiguous identity … .'[11]

The first railway line in Cuba was financed by the British, but built in 1837 by American engineers, who also introduced the steam engine and were responsible for some modernization of the sugar industry.

The Spanish monarchy responded to the increase in Cuba's black population by attempting to promote white immigration, particularly to the provincial towns. To this end they even offered inducements to those intending

to settle close to ports such as Nuevitas, Guantánamo and Jagua. Accordingly, at the beginning of the nineteenth century, a retired Lieutenant-Colonel Louis de Clouet of the Louisiana regiment obtained the concession of just over one thousand hectares in the Bay of Jagua, where he established a settlement of forty Spanish families. This was the beginning of the development of Cienfuegos, later to become one of the country's most important towns. Some of the original immigrants became influential merchants and made their fortune there. One of them, Tomás Terry, was responsible for building the town's splendid theatre.

Also in the nineteenth century Chinese workers were rapidly brought in to replace the African slaves in certain jobs after the suppression of the slave trade. They worked in increasing numbers on the plantations, as well as in the towns and villages. The coolies, as they were called, began work with an eight-year contract, but were in fact treated like slaves for the rest of their lives. Sometimes they were used to serve at table in the big houses. According to contemporary accounts they also found work in the sugar mills.

The new economic social distinctions

A population with such varied origins and customs created an identifiably Cuban culture that was inevitably a mixture of them all. Interestingly, and in contrast with English and French colonies in the Caribbean, most of Cuba's immigrants settled permanently, some even becoming big landowners, and did not go back to Europe to spend the money they had accumulated. In the course of time their families multiplied, and their children, born and bred in Cuba, intended to stay there all their lives. The Cuban whites, or Creoles, were some of the wealthiest inhabitants and had a very close attachment to the island. Most of them were of Spanish origin and constituted the country's aristocracy. They and the colonial government officials together formed the most privileged social class. At the beginning of the nineteenth century there were twenty-nine noble families, and a great many of them had never set foot in Spain. Some members of this Cuban aristocracy who were born on the island, like the Marqués de Arcos, the Conde de Fernandina and the Conde de Peñalver, owned the biggest plantations in the country and were thus also the principal sugar mill owners. The first-generation Spaniards from Europe could not accept their supremacy, calling them disdainfully the *sacarocracia* or 'sugar aristocrats'. But whether they liked it or not these same Creole members of the *sacarocracia* were responsible for the development of large enterprises and contributed significantly to the island's economic progress.

The aristocracy, dating from the eighteenth century, began to change in the

A simple house of wood and bricks at Baracoa. Houses like this were very common in the eastern coastal regions of the country from the middle of the nineteenth century onwards.

117

nineteenth century when the monarchy created new titles specifically for the recent immigrants. The old aristocracy retreated, scorning any connection with these newly created branches of the ruling class, who in turn looked down on the old established families. The Creoles had cut themselves off from Spain, resenting the new arrivals, who worked successfully in commerce and held some of the most influential posts in public life.

Next down the social scale after the aristocrats came the merchants, some of whom became very rich as a result of the sugar trade. As well as those of Spanish descent there were among them a considerable number of French, British, American and German traders. One of them was Tomás Terry who had established himself at Cienfuegos. He was one of the wealthiest men in the country and his business was so successful that its shares were quoted on the New York Stock Exchange.

The political antagonism between this new social class comprising merchants and large property owners and the old nobility that it was gradually replacing came to a head during the nineteenth century. The leaders of this new-style Spanish aristocracy were figures such as Joaquín Gómez and the Conde de Santovenia. Their position in the colonial power structure set them apart from the native Cuban bourgeoisie. Prominent people such as Domingo del Monte encouraged the intellectuals of the period to embrace a new vision of the future that would be compatible with the prevailing bourgeois and liberal mood.

The middle class, formed during the previous

Opposite: Calle Santa Ana in Trinidad.

Above: The dining-room in the house of the poet Regino Boti at Guantánamo.

119

century, became securely established through the economic and cultural developments of the early years of the new century. Many of its members made a notable contribution to the scientific and cultural developments of the period with their high reputation and intellectual authority.

The Cuban lifestyle

From the beginning of the nineteenth century Cubans had made a conscious effort to differentiate themselves from the Spaniards who lived in Spain. This marked drive to create a separate identity showed itself in a variety of ways in people's daily lives. Hitherto, for example, the merchants and peasants had drunk almost exclusively Catalan wine, the most widely available wine in the country. However, French 'clairette' (a light red wine) became increasingly popular, particularly with the richer families, who also began to change their eating habits. At the end of the century the traveller Samuel Hazard remarked on the subject: 'Since the dishes served at table in most of the towns, all the hotels and a good number of private houses are French, genuinely Cuban dishes can only be sampled in the rural areas.'[12]

This new attitude also affected the way in which people dressed. The rich Creoles stopped importing their clothes from Spain and had them sent from Paris or London. The most distinguished Havana ladies followed Parisian fashion, while the gentlemen adopted the English style. As a result, there were a large number of boutiques selling French fashions, mostly concentrated in the main

Below: Façade of the house built in the second half of the nineteenth century by the Catalan immigrant Gaudencio Boti, one of the founders of the town of Guantánamo. Two generations later the Cuban poet Regino Boti was born here. This type of house was very common in the small provincial towns – a single storey at street level, a little roofed porch with wooden posts and inside both a patio and a rear patio.

Opposite: The dining-room in the Boti house at Guantánamo, still inhabited by his descendants. The furniture of the period has been preserved. The chequered floor pattern, much used in the grandest homes, was often copied in more modest provincial houses.

streets of Havana. Some of the best known were those of Mme Bovés, Mme Pitaux and Mme Barber in Calle Obispo, who sold clothes and hats imported from their own countries or made by them in the French style.

In the nineteenth century it became popular to take refreshing fruit drinks rather than water, as well as wine, with both the midday and evening meal. At certain times of the day people in society liked to enjoy cool drinks of juice, usually made with oranges, limes or lemons. They also ate mangoes, and apricots from San Domingo, soursops, annonas and *chirimoyas* or custard apples, as well as papayas, known for their delicious fresh taste and digestive properties. There were also guavas, and pineapples with their distinctive shape and scent, which are thought to be one of the few fruits native to the island and the best of them all.

Of all this abundance of fruit, bananas and oranges were the most popular, often eaten during the morning before lunch, and they became the fruit most identified with the country. Other kinds were more seasonal and were used mostly for making juice to drink in the very hot weather. One particularly delicious and typically Cuban drink was *champola*, a mixture of soursop, sugar and milk.

Fruit trees were often used in ornamental planting in gardens and avenues. Coconut trees grew in towns and villages, as well as being a familiar sight in the countryside. Although very decorative, they were also prized everywhere for the delicious flesh of the fruit, and for the milk, which can be drunk through a hole in the nut.

Above all, people ate bananas. They soon became the peasants' daily food and were the main nourishment of the slaves and the poor in general, along with *tasajo*.[13] Prepared in a variety of different ways, they have always been a staple of the Cuban diet.

Hazard described the food available to people in the countryside: ' ... the daily meals of the most humble peasants consist of fried pork and boiled rice in the morning, fried and grilled bananas being eaten instead of bread. In the afternoon they eat beef, *tasajo* and grilled fish and pork; the most frequent meal is just grilled bananas and the national dish, *ajiaco*.'[14] Contemporary accounts describe the slaves' diet as even more restricted – they had rice, salt fish, smoked meat or *tasajo* and a few vegetables. ' ... they are fed with a kind of root called *malanga* which they appear to enjoy very much ... it is

Opposite: The Ministerio de Azúcar or Ministry of Sugar at Cienfuegos. The town was founded in 1819 by the Frenchman Louis de Clouet and is now the foremost sugar port in the world.

Left: Example of a *tinajero* at Trinidad. This system was widely used in Cuba to preserve drinking water. The water was filtered through porous stone and stored in a jar where it remained fresh.

Opposite: Bedroom of a house in Calle Amargura in Trinidad.

yellow, and very like the potato … Each slave is given a portion of these cooked roots, which they eat with salt beef. At midday, they are given boiled maize, which they crush and mix with wild tomatoes, bananas and vegetables … .'[15]

Both the blacks and the Chinese had their own ways of cooking and some of their recipes were eventually used by their masters. At this time *fufú* had the reputation of being the black slaves' favourite food – a kind of hard, highly flavoured pudding, made of pulped bananas and eaten with a tomato and vegetable sauce. Potatoes were rarely grown in Cuba, and many immigrants ate *fufú* instead, as did the Creoles. Root vegetables such as manioc and *malanga* were becoming an increasingly important part of their diet, and were eaten with butter or other fats. Many of these dishes, originally the core of the slaves' diet, became part of the Creole repertoire and are the basis of what is now considered to be traditional Cuban cuisine.

Until about 1820 Cubans drank chocolate rather than coffee. However, the 'black nectar', with or without milk, rapidly became the favourite. It was drunk first thing in the morning and after meals. According to the Cuban historian Pérez de la Riva, this change in tastes coincided with the new affirmation of Cuban nationality. Drinking black coffee and eating white rice with black beans was a way of being different from the Spaniards, who preferred chocolate, chick peas and paella.

Generally Cubans took a cup of coffee or chocolate immediately after rising, with only a small amount of toast or a biscuit, in anticipation of the large meal eaten at nine, ten or eleven in the morning. The wealthy classes would rise early, have a cup of their favourite hot drink and light a cigar before going out for a ride on horseback, or strolling in the patio and around the balconies. The family meal which followed was served with wine and included fruit, fish, meat, soup and eggs with ham. Among a great variety of desserts were those made with milk, fruit jellies or fruit in syrup. At all social levels the Cuban custom was to eat guava or coconut jam with cheese, which even today surprises many visitors.

Cigars were handed round with the dessert, and visitors were also intrigued to observe that they were lit from a little brazier of glowing coals, brought in by the servant at the same time as the coffee. Smoking had become widespread during the nineteenth century. People smoked in dining-rooms and drawing-rooms, but also on the trams, during theatre intervals and even in church doorways, according to a traveller at the time.

Around three o'clock another large meal was served, lasting about an hour. Everyone then retired for the siesta and at about five the carriage or *volanta* was brought out. Sometimes the young men and women were taken to see bulls racing, or else went to the promenades or *paseos*, one of the attractions of life in Havana at the time. Here they enjoyed having a stroll and doing some shopping in the early evening. This was also the time of day for paying calls, which followed a predictable pattern. 'In the main drawing room one can see rows of four or five chairs facing each other, against the wall. As one walks along the road, the families and their visitors can be seen taking their places

ceremoniously on these rows of chairs. Since the windows have large grilles but no glass and are therefore wide open, all Havana's drawing-rooms can be readily inspected, the ladies' clothes examined and their visitors observed.'[16]

At nightfall many kinds of carriages went up and down the fine avenues lined with palms and fruit trees, and rows of buildings that were gradually extended along both sides of the road. Beautiful young women displayed themselves as they passed in their *quitrines* (horse-drawn carriages with two wheels – a kind of cabriolet with a folding hood) or *volantas*, while gentlemen on horseback greeted them and, if the young women permitted it, came to pay their respects. The following describes the scene on the *paseos*: 'A private *volanta* goes back and forth, standing out with its rich silver decorations and the postilion in livery.... Most of them carry a gentleman, with a cigar in his mouth; in others, all one can see is a mass of blue or pink muslin or percale spilling out on to the carriage-shafts, surmounted by a fan, presumably hiding a lady's face.'[17] The *volanta* was the carriage mostly used by ladies and, since they were not permitted to walk in the streets alone, it allowed them to be seen on the *paseo* without getting out. They even made purchases by stopping their carriage in front of a shop and waiting for an assistant to come out and attend to them. Sometimes the shopkeepers would bring their newest stock to be examined by the ladies at home. In the main drawing room they would display dresses, hats and shoes for the elegant women to choose from. The striking shape of the carriages used by these ladies is described by the Swedish novelist and commentator Frederika Bremer in the 1850s: 'They are like large insects with enormous back legs and a long snout, with a big black tusk or protuberance shaped like a turret, moving around and threading their way in all directions. This was my first impression of the Cuban carriages or *volantas*, the only vehicles to be seen in Havana ....'[18]

The *volantas* and all other carriages were driven by a very elegantly dressed black *calesero* or coachman, in big turned-down top boots and decked out, like the horses pulling the coach, with impressive silver decorations. *Volantas* were to be observed on all the *paseos* of Havana

Opposite: This wrought-iron bedstead with applied decoration was probably imported.

Above: A sophisticated type of *tinajero* or water-filter, part of the collection of the Museum of Colonial Art in Havana.

and even in the provincial towns. It was common to see travelling in them 'two or three ladies, always hatless and sometimes with flowers in their hair, bare arms and necks, and dressed in white gauze dresses as if they were going to a ball … . They were often to be seen on the *paseos* in the afternoon, or in the Plaza de Armas in the evening, where music was playing and there were crowds of people … .'[19]

Following Havana's lead, promenading on the *paseos* became a favourite pastime in the other towns, and increasingly so as more and more tree-lined streets, avenues and parks were laid out. At the beginning of the century the only *paseos* in the capital were the Alameda de Paula and the Paseo de Isabel II. The Alameda was within the city walls near the port. The wide central drive for the carriages had parallel pathways with seats along either side and was lined with rows of trees. At one end of the avenue was the Coliseo, the first theatre to be built in Cuba, although it was never very successful. Eventually the people of Havana abandoned the Alameda and frequented instead the much more spacious and elegant *paseos* built outside the city at the beginning of the century.

As soon as it was laid out the Paseo de Isabel II (or Paseo del Prado) was a popular place to take a walk. Although it was built at much the same time as the *paseo* in the city, it attracted more visitors when the most distinguished residents of the city began to take their carriages

out beyond the city walls to enjoy the countryside. It became increasingly popular over the years and took pride of place over the Alameda. There were also many additional attractions, from benches for walkers to a variety of bands along the way. There was a great deal of new building in the district to cater for the taste for the spacious areas outside the city walls, confirming the pre-eminence of the Paseo del Prado.

The Paseo de Tacón (more often called the Paseo de Carlos III) was built shortly after the Paseo del Prado and was also much used by Havana high society for the sake of its ample proportions. Its straight avenues had two tracks for the carriages and two other pathways for pedestrians, separated by rows of trees. Fountains and statues were installed at intervals along the entire length of the avenue. It reached almost as far as the Castillo del Príncipe, where an imposing wrought-iron gate led into Havana's Botanical

Garden, and to the Quinta de los Molinos, the summer residence of the Captains-General.

At about five or six in the afternoon, people went to the *paseos* to promenade, drawn to the areas of the town where the welcome breezes were particularly refreshing. The Paseo del Prado was regarded in the nineteenth century as the most attractive of them all because of its excellent amenities. At the end of the century it ran from the Punta as far as the Tacón theatre. With its pavements, separate drives for the carriages and long rows of trees, it was the most popular of the *paseos*, particularly with Havana high society, because it was the nearest to the main gates of the city. After the walls had been demolished in 1865 the *paseo* marked the dividing line between the old town and the new. Magnificent new buildings lined the *paseo*. They were mostly private houses, with entrances in the fine arcades painted in traditional white or blue. The first hotels in Havana were built within reach of the *paseos*. In the nineteenth century the town was lacking in facilities for visitors, and they either stayed in family pensions or rented rooms in private houses. In the last decades of the century there were still only two hotels, the Pasaje and the Inglaterra. The Café El Louvre was very popular with young men, who went there every day to drink and talk together. But this café was more

Opposite and above: The Paseo del Prado, a tree-lined promenade outside the city walls, is the archetypal grand avenue and was used at carnival time for parades of decorated floats. The long rows of buildings on either side were erected in the early decades of the twentieth century. Apart from a few changes in decorative detail, the façades are very much in the old tradition, including the arcades which provide covered walkways for pedestrians.

than just a place of entertainment for some of the capital's male inhabitants: it was also the focus of political conspiracy.

A fine hotel, the Salón Trotcha, was built at the turn of the century in the El Vedado district, and became the most popular hotel in Cuba for honeymoon couples. Apart from these three purpose-built hotels, most others in the capital were in buildings converted from other uses. A conspicuous example is the Hotel Santa Isabel, which was established in the old residence of the Conde de Santovenia in the Plaza de Armas. After various setbacks it has recently been reopened. The Plaza de Armas (where the Palacio del Gobernador, or Governor's Palace, stands) was regarded as another fashionable place of relaxation. The garden with its scented flowers, paths and benches was a popular place to walk in at around eight o'clock in the evening and listen to the *Retreta* – a performance given by fifty or sixty musicians. The square was very animated both day and night. Nearby were the main government offices, and in other streets in the neighbourhood (Calle Oficios, Calle Mercaderes, Calle O'Reilly and Calle Obispo) were the town's most important shops, businesses and administrative offices. After six o'clock in the evening there was music in the square, making it a popular place of entertainment. It was, in addition, the only part of town where ladies were able to get out of their carriages and walk about freely.

For many of the capital's inhabitants, gambling and cock-fighting were popular daily pastimes. But what they enjoyed perhaps more than anything – and still do today – was dancing. According to contemporary records everybody danced, whatever their age or social class, from babies who had only just learned to walk to elderly women, from the Captain-General to the lowliest clerk. All over Cuba balls were the most usual form of celebration and a favourite entertainment. They were organized on the slightest pretext. Whether they were big, publicly arranged galas or took place in private houses among friends, dancing and watching others dance was a pastime enjoyed by everyone. For this reason music was always to be heard. In the streets, squares and private drawing-rooms there was always someone available to sing and play an instrument. This was a custom common to the whole country, as Frederika Bremer described after a visit to the town of Matanzas: '… my host's house is built on two floors. On the second, facing the street, is a balcony where I walk every evening to take the air, while my host's son plays Cuban quadrilles in the drawing-room … . The sound of these dances resonates on all sides from all the houses in the town. Wherever you go in Matanzas, you will hear dance music played … .'[20]

Other fashions came and went. Café life was increasingly enjoyed, particularly in the outlying areas of the city. A new departure was the therapeutic use of thermal baths, and soon afterwards sea bathing and summer holidays became common practice. As people began to see the benefits of bathing at the beaches, little wooden huts were put up so that ladies and their families could take to the water discreetly. It became the custom to spend part of the year by the sea in order to escape the suffocating heat of the old town.

Previous pages: The grounds of the Molinos del Rey, at the end of the Paseo del Tacón, were used to create the Botanical Gardens and the summer residence of the Captains-General, also called the Quinta de los Molinos. This long, wide avenue leading to the Quinta has gardens on both sides.

Opposite: Arcade of the Quinta de Santovenia in Havana, a residence in the neo-classical style situated in an outlying part of the city. In common with other buildings of its kind, it has a fine marble floor and splendid grilles and balustrades of wrought iron, which by now had comprehensively replaced the use of wood. This luxurious villa is surrounded by a garden with statues, fountains and a lake, on which guests could be rowed in gondolas when there was an evening party.

Opposite: Landowner's house in the Plaza del Carmen at Camagüey. Although the town is built on level ground, this long, single-storeyed house with a traditional roof is raised above street level and reached by a few steps. Houses in some of the nearby towns were built in the same way. The front door has two wicket openings with an undulating outline cut into it, and is flanked by two truncated pilasters, reaching only half way down the wall from the roof. The horizontal struts supporting the deep eaves add to the unusual appearance of the doorway.

Right: A house in Calle San Juan de Dios at Camagüey. The projecting window grilles are similar to those made in Trinidad in the same period. The terraced roof has a parapet decorated with inverted arches.

The provincial colonial house

The creation of towns and villages

Havana was not alone in benefiting from the economic expansion of the first half of the nineteenth century; it affected the whole country. Some of the provincial towns which became regional capitals enjoyed an unprecedented growth, greatly to the advantage of their economy and their culture. While the main focus of business and speculative activity was the capital, the agricultural and industrial production that earned smaller towns their prosperity was naturally centred on the provincial areas. The town of Matanzas, once known as the 'Athens' of Cuba, was typical. Trinidad, too, which became one of the most beautiful towns on the island, retains its original character and it is easy to imagine it in the time of general economic growth during which it prospered. Cienfuegos, Santiago de Cuba, Sancti Spíritus and Camagüey also possess reminders of that period. Far removed from the grandeur of some of the mansions in Havana, both the houses of the rich landowners and the humbler ones retained a certain austerity. Whether because it was situated so close to Havana or because it was developed so successfully, Matanzas was one of the towns most visited by foreigners in the nineteenth century. According to some of them, at

135

Above: The Palacio Junco in Calle Milanés at Matanzas was built between 1835 and 1840; it is an outstanding example of the town's nineteenth-century houses. Its arcades on both the ground and first floors are reminiscent of the eighteenth-century houses around the Plaza Vieja in Havana. At roof level is a parapet complete with ornamental urns – a typical feature of nineteenth-century Cuban colonial architecture.

Overleaf: Calle Amargura in Trinidad, the official route for religious processions and one of the town's most important thoroughfares. Some beautiful houses dating from the end of the eighteenth century and the beginning of the nineteenth are still standing. By contrast with Havana, wood has always been one of the most used materials here.

the beginning of the century it was 'built along the same lines as Havana, but had a freer, more lively atmosphere.'[21] The overall impression of the town was a cohesive one: 'The houses are fairly similar, all having only one floor, though some in the main streets are twenty feet high. The roofs are generally of plain tiles, occasionally pantiled, and some of the really old houses are roofed with palm leaves, like the ones in the country … .'[22]

Although some of the surrounding land was under cultivation by the end of the sixteenth century, Matanzas took a long time to profit from it and to begin to develop. It was not until free trade was established by the Spaniards in 1778 and a port was built in the bay of Matanzas in 1793 that the town was able to expand and start to build the reputation it enjoyed later. In spite of the wars and other problems that hindered its growth, the town managed to make some progress during the last years of the eighteenth century. In 1809 it was granted the right to trade with other countries, and from then on its position was secure. Sugar, coffee, honey, brandy and a variety of produce from the many estates, coffee plantations and cattle farms of the region were despatched from its large port. The town grew up around the port in the bay, and its subsequent expansion was one of the most significant of the century. It spread down the coast along a strip of well-watered land, where large houses lined the roads, and *quintas* or villas perched on the surrounding hillsides overlooking the port – always busy with shipping from Europe and the United States.

Most of the houses in Matanzas were built of wood and roofed with tiles (or occasionally with palm leaves). The wide, straight streets were well laid out, although they were not paved and had no drainage. Originally just a hamlet, as it grew the town kept in touch with architectural developments in Havana. The luxuriant vegetation all around and the variety of the scenery contributed greatly to its character.

Matanzas had a number of similarities with the capital. Its own Plaza de Armas is almost exactly the same shape and size as Havana's, and is one of the most attractive places in the country in which to go for a stroll. Because of its proximity to Havana and its own increasing prosperity, Matanzas was always the first town in Cuba to imitate developments in the capital.

The houses of Matanzas were well adapted to the climate and conditions. Many contemporary travellers noted their generous size, their efficient ventilation and their elegant simplicity. An American, the Rev. Abiel Abbott, writing in the 1820s made a point of mentioning the question of ventilation: 'I will describe to you the house of a friend of mine, a beautiful example of its kind. From the street, you come

137

straight into a square space, part of which is used to store a large rustic carriage called a *volanta*, which is pulled by a single horse; the other part is the entrance hall to the rest of the house. The main reception room also faces the street, and has two enormous windows fifteen feet high from the top of the frame to the bottom – big enough to let through the *volanta*. Instead of glass panes there is an iron grille or wooden bars. When the ladies can be seen behind them, they look like cloistered nuns. As the enormous windows reach nearly to the ground, the family practically lives on the street; whether they are in the middle of eating, working or amusing themselves, talking seriously or joking, whether in good or bad company, they are exposed to public scrutiny. However, sometimes they use the protection of the shutters … . Through the door is the patio, open to the skies. To the right and left are the bedrooms, and opposite is the kitchen.'[23]

The Casa de Gobierno was one of the largest buildings. The Casa de Junco and similar

Left: Although there are some fine landowners' houses in Trinidad, most of the town's dwellings are like the one shown here, standing at the corner of Calle Real de Jigue and Calle Desengaño – very plain, single-storey buildings with tiled roofs, built at street-level without gaps between them, along well-maintained roads.

houses were always situated near the main square. Fine villas or *quintas* were built on the outskirts of the town. These usually consisted of a single storey at street level, but some of the more imposing buildings took their cue from the large houses built in Havana at the time. For example, the Casa de Junco in the Plaza de Colón was built with a ground floor, a first floor with a gallery and a colonnade below.

It must be emphasized that it was above all the merchants in Matanzas who quickly became wealthy. Their homes reflected their way of life, as is well described by the American historian Roland T. Ely: 'The merchants always conducted their business at home, and as there were no banks in Cuba, they all had a metal safe to keep their money in; the stores of sugar, coffee and so on were next to the office. The merchant and his employee lived as a family, under the same roof and eating at the same table … .'[24]

Above: A house in Calle San José in Trinidad, one of many surviving eighteenth-century dwellings in this street. They are mostly low-built, with tiled roofs, plain eaves and a large doorway with windows of the same size on either side. The iron grilles which replaced the wooden ones in the nineteenth century have radically changed the appearance of this house.

Right: Crossroads of two of the oldest streets in Trinidad – Calle Alameda and Calle Media Luna. Their characteristic paving is designed to allow rainwater to run away.

The area around Trinidad consists of some of the roughest terrain on the island and the town itself is surrounded by mountains. The fertile Valle de los Ingenios – so named because of the large number of plantations there in the nineteenth century – is an exception in this part of the country. Although Trinidad was one of the first towns founded by Diego Velázquez, it took a long time to prosper. The situation improved when Trinidad started to trade illegally with Jamaica and with the Dutch in neighbouring islands. This smuggling was of great benefit to the areas in which it thrived. It boosted sugar production and cattle rearing, and gave rise to new commercial ventures. The situation was similar at Santiago de Cuba and other towns in central and eastern parts of the country, where illicit trade was an integral part the economy. Growth in these areas was most notable at the end of the eighteenth century, and particularly at the beginning of the nineteenth when French émigrés from Saint Domingue (Haiti) settled in the neighbourhood, and became managers of *cafetales* and *ingenios*.

Trinidad was built on the side of a hill called Loma de la Vigía, and the sloping site gave the nineteenth-century town the appearance of an amphitheatre. The highest point in the district is the hill called la Popa, which overlooks the town. The streets of Trinidad built on the slopes were steep and winding, except for those in the centre, which were laid out on a more regular plan. Most were paved, and stayed dry and clean; hygiene was much better than in Havana. The town's present excellent state of preservation bears witness to the ingenuity of the original builders, who took into account the irregularities of the terrain, particularly when laying out the squares and planning the construction of the houses.

This capacity to adapt to the conditions of the site, which is already clear from the outside of the house, can be seen in the organization of the rooms: the unusual contours affected the planning of the internal spaces as well. In these houses functional characteristics were combined with a very individual charm and the relationship between the architecture and the lie of the land was a determining factor.

The beautiful Plaza Mayor (or Plaza Fernando VII) in the centre of the town had to be built by adjusting to the sloping land. As in Havana, people came to the main square to walk and sit on the benches in the gardens.

Façade of the Casa Ortiz, built around 1809. Ortiz, one of the richest men in Trinidad, made his fortune as a slave trader and later invested in the sugar industry. The house stands at the corner of Calle Real de Jigue and Calle Desengaño and looks on to the Plaza Mayor. The walls are smooth and painted and, exceptionally for Trinidad, the upper floor has a long balcony running along the two façades. It is now the Guamuhaya Archaeological Museum.

143

Above: Patio of the Casa de Padrón in Trinidad. Standing in the Plaza Mayor, it dates from the eighteenth century, although it was much changed in the nineteenth. Many of the region's old families lived in this house where, in the town's heyday, they received important visitors such as the German explorer Baron Alexander von Humboldt.

Opposite: Patio of the Palacio Brunet, also in Trinidad's Plaza Mayor. Two different kinds of galleries can be seen. Since there was not room for four arched galleries, two of them were built with additional pitched roofs and supported on horizontal brackets, which avoided using space in the patio for load-bearing columns.

Overleaf: The original kitchen in the Palacio Brunet in Trinidad is one of the few to have survived. It is on the first floor and is tiled with terracotta squares. It has a large hood over the range. Decorative glazed tiles around the cooking area provided hygienic working conditions.

Many of the original houses survive as evidence of the prosperity of the town at the time. The Casa de Ortiz, the Casa de Padrón, the Palacio Cantero and the Palacio Brunet, all large and elegantly designed residences, are striking examples of Trinidad's architecture.

Wood was a prominently used material in all these houses, both for the ceilings and for outside decoration. Although it was replaced by iron for nearly all architectural details in Havana, wood continued to be of primary importance in Trinidad. In the capital the columns on the street façades were a unifying feature of the urban landscape. In Trinidad the carved wooden grilles on the windows, standing out from the plain walls of the houses ranged along the main streets, had the same effect. Moreover, in contrast to houses in Havana, there was no wall separating the dining-room from the drawing-room. Instead there were archways between them, making the rooms both more convenient

Left: A wrought-iron grille at a cobbler's workshop in Trinidad.

Above: Turned wood grilles and (*overleaf*) wrought-iron grilles in Trinidad.

Opposite and above: Interior of the Palacio de Justo Cantero, one of the most famous sights of Trinidad. It is a single-storey building, constructed between 1828 and 1830. Because of its impressive scale, the great height of the ceilings and the richness of the materials used for its neo-classical decorative scheme, it is regarded as one of the most luxurious buildings of its period. Today it houses the town's Historical Museum.

to use and more attractive. Both the improved circulation of air inside the house and the carefully chosen furniture added to the appeal of these houses.

During the course of the nineteenth century Trinidad began to lose its powerful position when the neighbouring town of Cienfuegos was greatly enlarged, having for a long time been only a village housing a small garrison responsible for its defence. About the middle of the seventeenth century fortifications had been built at the entrance to the bay of Jagua in an attempt to deflect the frequent incursions by the English, who used to put in along the coast in order to refit their ships. The port's hinterland was not extensively colonized, however, until the arrival of Louis de Clouet in the area, together with thousands of immigrants, between 1819 and 1822. More than half of these first settlers were foreigners, both Spanish and French. Later many Americans came to join them. The town was laid out on a fairly regular grid, with the streets forming right angles, the solidly built houses stretching from the Plaza to the Bay. The Plaza Principal, with its lovely gardens, paths and many statues, was to be one of the biggest and most impressive squares on the island.

Santiago, like the other towns in the eastern part of Cuba, had long periods of stagnation. At the end of the eighteenth century, however, it began a noticeable revival. Although its port was less busy than Havana's or the port at Matanzas, Santiago was enlarged and embellished after the arrival of all kinds of craftsmen in considerable numbers. At the same time French immigrants transformed the surrounding land into fertile estates and brought about a rapid expansion in production and trade. However, the streets, built on steep hillsides, were badly affected by rain and the lack of pavements made getting about very difficult. In Santiago the terrain was perhaps even more uneven than in Trinidad, although the architectural solutions adopted in both places were similar. Carved wooden windows projected from the street façades, and the balconies were a vantage point for the young girls both to be seen and to observe the passers-by.

Although the ways in which they decorated their houses varied, the provincial towns followed the same general layout. The focus was the main square (Plaza de Armas), where the colonial administration was based. This included the *ayuntamiento* (town hall), the church and the *cuartel* (barracks). Even more so than in the capital, the main square was the centre of social life, both for the inhabitants of the town and for those of the surrounding villages.

Drawing-room of the Palacio Brunet in Trinidad. Its notable features are the wooden ceiling, marble floor and painted dados. Such houses were family homes, but were also used a great deal for entertaining. The rooms were therefore of a generous size and were meticulously furnished and decorated.

Apart from certain local features, most dwellings followed the pattern of houses built in Havana. Frederika Bremer particularly noted this at Cárdenas – a little town on the coast near Matanzas with a considerable trade in sugar and syrup. It was founded in 1828 and a large number of American merchants made it one of the most prosperous towns on the island. It was built on a regular plan, with wide streets and, of course, a central square and had almost as many amenities as the little towns around Havana.

Frederika Bremer describes Guanabacoa, renowned for its therapeutic baths, as 'a miniature Havana; the houses are built and painted in the same way, with the same roofs and the same terraces with their decorative urns, but all on a smaller scale.'[25]

Generally speaking, places outside Havana – even those where rich landowners lived – were hardly more than villages. Frederika Bremer

The old families of Trinidad had become extremely rich during the first decades of the nineteenth century, and frequently had their furniture brought over from Europe or the United States. Many of these imported pieces were copied by local craftsmen and were to be seen in all Cuba's most opulent homes. Examples are displayed in the Museo Romántico in Trinidad, where mural paintings from reception rooms in the Palacio Brunet are also now preserved.

depicts them as composed largely of 'wonderful little blue and yellow houses, with little gardens full of brightly coloured flowers and unfamiliar plants, and some huts covered with palm leaves.'[26]

Another observer describes the town of Unión de Reyes (so called because it is at the junction of two main railway lines, and therefore an important staging post) as nothing but 'an impoverished hamlet. There are no large houses or anything of significance .... Although it is a provincial capital, it seems more like just a shelter for blacks and muleteers. The houses are like low, windowless stables, built with rough planks of wood, in which men and beasts huddle together in the same mud and poverty ... . These squalid shacks are painted on the outside in very bright colours – sky blue, emerald green, brick red, mustard yellow – in keeping with the taste of the inhabitants for crude decoration. There are some more attractive ones with a kind of covered gallery, raised on simple columns; the residents sit in its shade during the hottest hours of the day ... .'[27]

In the country and on the outskirts of villages the peasants still made their houses with palm leaves, as did the original inhabitants of the island. Such huts were usually built low and small in order to withstand hurricanes and the *mal tiempo* (as the rainy season is called in Cuba) which would otherwise have destroyed them. These little dwellings, usually built with walls of bark or interwoven dried twigs, remained the most usual kind of habitation for Cuban peasants for a long time to come.

The plantations

Apart from the magnificent residences of the plantation owners in the towns nearest to their estates (such as Trinidad, Matanzas or Cienfuegos), the most notable houses in the rural areas were in the *ingenios* and the *cafetales*, among the buildings used for processing the sugar and coffee. Although undoubtedly important, these houses did not match the grandeur of those in town. It must be emphasized that the wealthy owners of the *ingenios* and *cafetales* did not make their homes in the places that earned them their fortunes. These houses were used as 'pied-à-terres'[28] when they came to inspect the work on their estates.

A traveller at the time recorded that 'The master's house was not very different from the industrial buildings around it. The main part of the house looks on to the whole *batey* or works ... . It is of a single storey, only two steps up from ground level. It has a simple verandah running round all sides, with a few bamboo chairs, and shaded by the deep eaves of the roof.... Inside is a large room with roughly whitewashed walls, with a piano in one corner, a desk, a work-table, two cane sofas, a few armchairs and a few books ... . These incongruous and functional pieces of furniture seem lost in such a big, empty room ... . Only one thing matters: to be in the shade and to have unlimited space and air ... . The dining-room is an extension of the drawing-room, screened from it by a solid wall, but the two rooms intercommunicate via a door which is always kept open and two

Previous pages, left: Interior of a house in Trinidad, showing the characteristic neoclassical moulding on the door architrave and the type of cane chairs that were imported by families in Trinidad to add style to their homes.

Previous pages, right: Loggia used as a dining-room by the original inhabitants of the Palacio Brunet. As in the Casa de Ortiz, the arches overlooking the patio have been filled in with wooden shutters and fanlights.

Opposite: The Trinidad Historical Museum in the Palacio Cantero has furnished this bedroom with pieces from its large contemporary collection. The predominance of painting in the decorative scheme can be seen in the smallest details. The doors and ceilings have shell-shaped recesses above them, painted with motifs that are repeated throughout the house.

waist-height windows with iron grilles … . To the left, the private rooms of the master and his wife are closed off by cotton curtains, which are stirred by the wind.'[29]

The *ingenio* itself, by contrast, was made up of a variety of different structures. There were extensive buildings for the industrial production of sugar, as well as the employees' living quarters, the huts of the slaves and many other outbuildings, so that the establishment was like a complete village. For example the *ingenio* San Martín – the largest in Cuba – near Cárdenas was reportedly laid out like a typical Spanish village, with a symmetrical central square and roads leading off at right angles from each corner. 'The *ingenio* and the infirmary were the most impressive of the buildings facing this vast open space … . To the right of the *ingenio* are the slaves' living quarters or *barracón*. On the southern side of the square are the houses of the manager of the *ingenio*, the engineers and the *maestro de azúcar* (the overseer of all the phases of sugar production), the hospital and the fine gardens which extend for hundreds of feet behind it.'[30] In all the Cuban *ingenios* the buildings connected with sugar production were known collectively as the *batey*. They followed much the same layout, though some were larger than others. Permanent features were the foreman's and machine supervisor's houses, the infirmary, the kitchen, the *casa de purga*, the boiler-house, the sugar mill, the slaves' quarters, the master's house and even a tile-making workshop. All this added up to impressive establishments of considerable size, described by many visitors at the time. The *barracón* at any of these establishments could house up to four hundred slaves and was built in much the same way at all the large *ingenios*: 'The *barracón* consists of a walled enclosure, with a big door on one side which is closed at night. Inside are the slaves' homes – one room for each family – with a door leading on to the central patio. On the outside all that can be seen is a row of tiny barred windows, too small for the slaves to see out of. In the middle of the big patio is a building containing the kitchen, wash-house, etc.'[31]

On a few of the plantations the slaves were housed in *bohíos* of wood or palm leaves built near the *ingenios*, rather than in *barracones*. The Chinese workforce often lived separately, and were

sometimes allowed to build their huts in their own way. In areas where they could find bamboo and rushes, there are reports that they built in a Chinese style.

Poor peasants living independently of the plantations occupied dwellings which were much the same as the traditional *bohíos*. These primitive structures 'were built with wooden posts, palm leaves and bushy branches, in such a way that air was able to circulate, but the rain was kept out. The doors were always open … . Only an awning separated the living quarters from the kitchen, where the women prepared the meals and dealt with other domestic tasks.'[32] After the *ingenios* or sugar mills, the *cafetales* or coffee plantations were the other large establishments in the Cuban countryside. Here the *batey* consisted of mills, drying chambers, warehouses, an infirmary and the master's house. The coffee plantations have gradually disappeared, partly because of the hurricanes which severely damaged or completely destroyed them in the 1940s, but above all because of competition from the expansion of coffee growing in Brazil and on other islands in the West Indies. Subsequently, the *cafetales* were not reinstated but were adapted for sugar production. Unfortunately, there now remains hardly a trace of either *ingenios* or *cafetales*, since most of the sugar mills were also either destroyed by fire during the wars of independence or disappeared during the reorganization of the Cuban agricultural system.

The Palacio del Valle at Cienfuegos was built at the end of the nineteenth century by a Spanish millionaire. The extraordinary architectural style is a mixture of Gothic, Venetian and Moorish motifs.

Above: No. 51 Calle Heredia, one of the main streets in Santiago de Cuba. The house dates from the end of the eighteenth century and the beginning of the nineteenth. Although in poor condition, it still has its original long balcony and iron balustrade (iron was in common use in Santiago earlier than elsewhere).

Opposite: Street façade of the Palacio del Valle at Cienfuegos.

Opposite: A building in Calle O'Reilly in old Havana, with a shop on the ground floor and living-quarters above.

Right: Long balconies such as this one in Avenue Máximo Gómez y Rayo are a particular feature in the outer areas of Havana. The delicacy of the wrought-iron decoration shows the skill and creativity of the craftsmen of the time.

Havana in the nineteenth century

Urban developments

As the number of inhabitants and the pace of building in Havana increased during the nineteenth century, the contrast between the capital and the other towns on the island became more marked. Commercial activity and administrative responsibilities multiplied as Havana's role as capital of the colony was strengthened. New public institutions needed new premises to work from. As a result a great variety of buildings were erected both within and outside the city walls in response to the changing needs of the time. Among them were markets, prisons, theatres and luxurious houses, all part of a process of modernization which radically altered the appearance of the town. The familiar image of Havana as an old city, enclosed within high walls, was now firmly in the past. New building continued throughout the century and the enlargement of the capital also led to improvements in public amenities.

By the end of the nineteenth century, one of the richest and most complex in its history, Havana had undergone a remarkable transformation. At the beginning, however, it was still a relatively small town.

A contemporary visitor described his first impression of the port in these words: 'The town of Havana, like nearly all towns in the Antilles, is built on a flat shore within a bay. Approaching the town from the sea, one sees a narrow opening, with a rocky promontory to the left of it, surmounted by a fortress called El Morro … which stands out with a noble and commanding air. On the right-hand side … there is a little fort called La Punta, less attractive and less powerful than El Morro. A ship patrolling the gap between the two calls out and demands to know the name and port of origin of all craft – the narrowness of the entrance makes it possible to communicate in this manner. After that, one can enter the port … . On the right-hand shore, behind La Punta, the stone buildings of Havana can now be seen, among them the numerous bell-towers of churches and convents, all within the city's enclosing walls.'[33]

Left: View of the Calle Guarabo in Havana. This sloping street used to lead right down to the river of the same name.

Opposite: Calle San Martín in Havana.

At this time the core of the city was still the part contained within the walls (known as the *casco antiguo*) and most of the population lived in this small area bounded by the sea and the ramparts. The city's grid-like plan was established from the beginning, and the narrow streets, as in medieval towns, were designed to protect the inhabitants from frequent attack from outside. In spite of the necessarily defensive character of the majority of its buildings, the small colonial town also possessed much charm, with its large squares, little parks and open spaces where roads intersected. These less imposing areas were in their own way just as attractive as the beautiful wide *paseos* which were later so characteristic of the areas immediately outside the walls. At the beginning of the century the streets were already very crowded, and the old city presented many practical problems. Some foreign visitors remarked on the 'crystal clear' quality of the air, probably because they came from towns polluted by smoke from factories; others, however, expressed astonishment that 'the roads are by no means wide, though this should be a priority in such a crowded city, where life is impossible without the refreshing effect of the sea breezes. The American ladies never permit themselves to set foot on the uneven, often wet streets of the city … .'[34]

It is certainly true that Havana generally was in a poor state of repair. The difficulties caused by the narrowness of the streets were increased by the inadequate road surfacing and in some cases the complete absence of paving. At the very beginning of the century renewed efforts were made to improve the condition of the roads. Paving stones were laid for the first time, but were not used consistently before the end of the century. Some stretches of road were asphalted – an improvement on previous

attempts to deal with the problem, which had left the roads still in a deplorable state. Paving stones and asphalt gradually replaced other road surfaces, which had been damaged by the heat and heavy rain. These difficulties were not finally resolved until the beginning of the twentieth century, when road maintenance and the establishment of a proper drainage system were undertaken jointly.

In Havana there were no areas inhabited exclusively by the upper classes. Their houses were mostly scattered over a number of streets, being grouped together only in the city's squares. One traveller noted that 'although the roads are laid out in evenly spaced straight lines, the buildings within the grid are extremely varied. For example, it is possible to find a poor and dilapidated house next door to a sumptuous palace, or the oldest and most impractical structure next to one that is the height of modernity and elegance ... .'[35] Although the town within the walls was in many ways inconvenient, the people living there had learned to adapt to the climate and to provide themselves with certain comforts. Some of the shopkeepers made use of the narrowness of the streets to stretch great awnings from one side to the other, thus sheltering pedestrians from both the heat and the heavy rain. These tarpaulins, often very brightly coloured, were draped across the busiest shopping streets and considerably enlivened the appearance of the town.

In contrast with the old walled city, the new Havana which began to emerge during the nineteenth century was provided with wide roads and vast avenues. It was much easier to move around here than in the old town, the congestion in its narrow streets making daily life very uncomfortable. Right up to the nineteenth century Havana had hardly spread beyond its enclosing walls. The growth which it had enjoyed at the end of the eighteenth century as a result of its economic expansion changed its character and impelled it to develop on the far side of the walls. The unsystematic early extensions showed that it was imperative to plan the outer zone properly in order to control the development of the town. The *paseos* were laid out with this in mind, as were some residential avenues or *calzadas*, such as the Avenida Reina and the Avenida Belascoaín. The system used in the *casco viejo* was abandoned in the planning of these new areas, and the roads were aligned along two basic axes – one to the northwest and the other to the southwest – in order to simplify the expansion of the town.

In this outer zone there were both large palatial houses and very humble dwellings. The diversity of the buildings put up here endowed Havana with a new personality. Developers were drawn to this part of the town to build theatres, hotels and dance-halls, all of which needed considerable space and would have been much more expensive to build within the city walls.

A number of modern innovations affected the city as it developed, among them the construction of the first railway lines – the first stretch of all was built to link Havana with the neighbouring village of Bejucal. This new transport system obviously greatly improved communication with the agricultural areas, and new villages were built and developed at intervals along the route taken by the railway.

Until the middle of the nineteenth century the vehicles most used by those who could afford them were still the *quitrines* and the *volantas*. However, a great variety of other kinds of carriages were soon to be seen all over the capital. In addition to the traditional ones, new four-wheeled, horse-drawn carriages called *victorias* came into use. These had several seats, and were often hired by tourists and other visitors.

Opposite: One of old Havana's narrow streets, the tall buildings forming a densely packed single row.

Opposite: The Quinta (villa) del Marqués de Pinar del Río in the El Cerro district of Havana.

During the nineteenth century great changes took place in the capital which profoundly altered its appearance and the way of life of its inhabitants. Nevertheless, in spite of the impact of alteration and expansion, Havana was still really a large village. It was only in the first decade of the twentieth century that it became a rich and elegant city.

Houses as status symbols

Until the nineteenth century houses in the towns were rarely of more than a single storey and never more than two. Only in Havana, where very large houses had been built for the Creole aristocracy in previous centuries, were there were some with two or occasionally three storeys, including the mezzanine floor. Even in Havana houses most often had only a single floor and were of much the same type as those in the rural areas, the humbler dwellings outnumbering the grand ones.

In residential districts such as El Horcón or Jesús María, with the exception of a few stone-built dwellings the houses were constructed of wooden planks, palm leaves and earth. The buildings near the city walls and in the areas beginning to be developed outside the walls were much the same, and it was common to see 'low houses painted in many colours – blue, yellow, green and orange – like a vast array of multicoloured glasses and china in a gift shop .... Clumps of palm trees were scattered among the houses.'[36]

The characteristic medium-sized houses predominated in the city, but there were others whose design was different from either the traditional Spanish or Creole ones and which made a significant contribution to the diversity of Havana's architecture. In the early years of the nineteenth century visitors had noticed a number of houses reminiscent of those in the southern and southeastern American states. Trade between the United States and Cuba was beginning to develop at this time and the German explorer Baron Alexander von Humboldt remarked on American influence on house design: 'The land from La Punta to San Lazaro, from La Cabana to Regla and from there to Atarés is covered with houses; those around the Bay are of a light and elegant construction. They have been built by drawing an outline plan and *ordering* a design from the United States as if one was ordering a piece of furniture.'[37]

Although most of the houses in Havana continued to be single-storey with stone walls and tile roofs, the dramatic changes that took place in the design of the homes of wealthy families had an undeniable impact on the appearance of the city, which impressed itself upon visitors to Havana even at the beginning of the century: 'Seen from the port, the town presents an air of rather decayed grandeur; the maritime comings and goings give it interest; there is an overriding impression of riches and luxury .... The narrow streets are lined with solidly built houses.'[38]

Since the richest families in the country lived in Havana, a large number of mansions and fine houses were built there as the urban expansion continued. Their inhabitants were members of the old Creole aristocracy, a few rich merchants and officials of the colonial administration. Although their residences to some extent followed the traditional pattern, the introduction of new elements to satisfy contemporary demands contributed to the development of a specifically Creole kind of house. Those families who had become rich as a result of the country's rapid expansion in industry and commerce began to surround themselves with an ever-increasing number of material comforts. Their large, even ostentatious, houses became the outward signs of their social pre-eminence.

Houses in the old town

New houses built within the city walls continued to follow the classic plan of the eighteenth-century buildings around the main squares, since their owners wanted to preserve the outward appearance of the older neighbour-hoods. The introduction of many typically Cuban elements (such as the *azotea* or roof terrace) was part of the gradual evolution of colonial houses. At the beginning of the nineteenth century the façades of the houses inhabited by the upper and middle classes still retained the relatively simple design of their predecessors. The wide doorway (placed either to one side or centrally), broad enough for a *volanta* to pass through, was gradually enlarged, but the general plan of the house remained the same. In fact, such houses can sometimes be mistaken for eighteenth-century ones, with their enormous ground-floor rooms, their wide, high, grilled windows on each floor and their balconies running the entire width of the house. Inside, the space continued to be organized around the central patio. The ground floor was enlarged to allow for the increasing commercial use of the building. A mezzanine reserved for offices and domestic matters became much more common, and the first floor or '*piano nobile*' continued to be for the exclusive use of the family. The important difference was that the scale of the building, the materials used and the quality of all the details transformed these houses into mansions.

The merchants' houses all followed a pattern. One report noted: 'The entrances are very spacious, the staircases as regal as those in Stafford House in London [known today as Lancaster House], the floors are marble, the walls are covered in *azulejos* or small glazed tiles and the banisters are made of iron. The rooms are twenty feet high, with exposed beams, the doors and windows are huge, the furniture is elaborate and solidly made. Here the merchant or banker sits, in white trousers and elegantly shod. He undoes his white jacket, loosens his tie and smokes cigars, surrounded by luxury and sheltered from the sun.'[39]

A number of these residences can still be seen today, although some are in a bad state of repair. They are reminders of the living standards, tastes and customs of the rich at that period. Two representative examples are the houses of Don José Ricardo O'Farrill (between the Calle Cuba and the Calle Chacón), and of Don Joaquín Ríos between the Calle Habana and the Calle Chacón. The latter is today the Bishop's Palace.

The juxtaposition of gracious residences with dilapidated outbuildings often surprised visitors, and it was not unusual to find a *quitrín* stabled next to an immaculate drawing-room or a merchant's stock stored near the large, elegantly furnished rooms used by members of the family. The shrewd observer Frederika Bremer described these contrasting conditions: 'Next to a lovely arcade and well-painted wall there can be another wall in a very decrepit condition, with fresco paintings all but obliterated, or even crumbling away along with the plaster ... .'[40]

In houses with an upper floor the space behind the street arcade and the imposing front door (the *zaguán*) could be used for the carriage. Beyond that were the storerooms for the owner's stock and household goods (although sometimes these spaces were let to others for the same purpose). The private upper floor was separated from the rest of the house by increasingly grand flights of stairs.

There were a large number of retail businesses in Havana, and the owners of houses with several storeys often let sections of the ground floor to shop-keepers. This part of Joaquín Ríos' luxurious residence was used by many commercial enterprises and visitors found it hard to believe that the possessors of a vast fortune lived on the floor above this scene of intense activity. Bemused foreign visitors were usually reassured by the presence of an elegantly dressed porter.

Another important factor in the history of Havana's houses was the

inevitable gradual increase in the value of land in the walled part of the city, which often resulted in the addition of a second or even third storey to some buildings in order to make the most profitable use of them.

In keeping with tradition, the entrance continued to be the principal decorative element of the façades of buildings. The increasingly imposing doors were resplendent with bronze details (such as the nails, door-knockers and hinges) which greatly added to the whole effect.

After the door and the entrance hall, a small vestibule led first to the staircases and then directly into the patio which served as a garden and was a source of cooler air, even on the hottest days. Frederika Bremer describes approvingly the well-ventilated loggias around the patio, built first on two of its sides and later on all four. They provided large, sheltered spaces for a variety of domestic uses. At this period there were blinds or coloured canopies to protect the house from the heat of the sun or the bad weather, and the loggias could be used as dining or living areas. They became an essential part of family life: '… the inhabitants come and go, and live in full view of everyone. They dine and receive visitors there; the lady of the house sews and attends to her children, surrounded by her slaves. The servants do the washing and deal with other domestic matters – all this takes place in the open loggias where people and the air circulate with equal freedom.'[41]

Previous pages: Wheel-guards on doorways in old Havana.

Left and above left: In all the towns particular attention was paid to the huge doorways. Apart from their size, the superior quality of the wood and their patterned studs, many of them are also remarkable for their wheel-guards or buffers, which are minor works of art.

Opposite: Entrance to the Casa Simón Bolívar, Havana.

The loggias usually had marble floors, and large internal doors led from the loggias into the bedrooms. In single-storey houses the windows looking on to the street were protected by wooden or metal grilles. The windows on the first floor obviously allowed more privacy, but were also protected by grilles. When more houses were built with an upper floor, staircases became an important feature. At first they were built in stone, and later in marble. The private areas of the building were now on the upper floor and the decoration of the staircase was designed to be in keeping with this suite of rooms.

Windows were increasingly large and were always left open. Because of the climate they had no glass panes and passers-by could easily watch what was happening inside. Only the wooden or metal grilles prevented entry by undesirable intruders, but the residents were by no means averse to being observed. Although the grilles had a purely practical function, they were also the focus of particularly elaborate decoration. These 'highly worked' screens allowed those standing on the outside to admire 'the beautiful young women in their rocking-chairs, cooling themselves with brightly coloured fans.'[42]

Little balconies were soon built outside the first-floor windows, creating a link with the street. Eventually these individual balconies were joined up to run right across the façade and played an important part in the family's social life. They permitted an interchange between the inside and outside of the colonial house and soon consolidated the habit of almost living in the street. Balconies quickly became an integral part of the façades. Their decoration and the details of the balustrades depended on the materials available to the builders and on the prevailing stylistic influences of the period.

The more houses that were built, the closer they were together and it became essential to mark boundaries. Highly decorated *guardavecinos* were erected. These were grilles designed to separate the balconies, and became so commonplace on street façades that they very soon formed an essential element of the urban landscape, particularly in the old town and neighbouring areas.

The heights of roofs had greatly increased during previous centuries, but became even higher in the course of the nineteenth century. The extra space which this created, combined with the increased size of the patio, allowed good ventilation even on the hottest days of the year. The form of the roofs changed, too, in accordance with the tastes and

Opposite: When long, continuous balconies began to be widely installed, it became necessary to fit *guardavecinos* – grilles made to separate neighbours' balconies from one another.

Above: Calle San Martín in old Havana.

Mampara or door-screen in the Quinta del Marqués de Pinar del Río in Havana.

fashions of the time, and *azoteas* or flat terraces began to replace the older, pitched ones. Inside, the *mudéjar*-style open roofs, linked to traditional Spanish architecture, were abandoned in favour of the new taste for plastered ceilings. From the nineteenth century onwards new stylistic models took precedence, and in both mansions and more modest dwellings ceilings were built showing the specific influence of European architectural trends. Although these features were already a little out of date, they brought the required modern touch to Cuban houses: '… everywhere there were flat roofs with stone or metal parapets, and urns with flames of bronze.'[43] *Azoteas* were very popular on hot summer evenings. People went there to smoke, talk and often to listen to music, enjoying the cooler evening air. Frederika Bremer has this description: 'My bedroom and a few of the other rooms have access to the terrace, which is very pleasant for me, as I can go there at any time to take the air. I need only to climb a little staircase to be on the *azotea*. It is an extremely important part of the house, where Cuban families gather in the evening to take advantage of the breeze.'[44]

Floors were generally laid with marble, always clean and shining and without carpets, in order to keep the rooms cool. In the grander houses the reception rooms were used to hold dances for groups of friends. Often there were 'two kinds of rocking chairs placed near the windows, some of a Spanish design, the others American … one could sit there and chat while rocking and fanning oneself in the breeze from the window.'[45]

Again, as a contemporary commentator recorded, there was not much furniture. 'Valuable houses worth fifty or one hundred thousand pesos nevertheless only have half a dozen of the mahogany and cane armchairs which they call rocking chairs … and ten or twelve very small chairs around the lamp in the middle of the room. Apart from a few exceptions, all the houses of Havana have a room furnished in this way.'[46]

A particularly Cuban piece of furniture was the *estelladora* (sometimes also called a *tinajero*) which was used to store fresh drinking water; its design took different forms according to the relative affluence of the household. Inside it was a container, 'a kind of large jar which was, and still is, made from porous clay … . It was used all over Cuba to keep houses supplied with fresh water. The water was filtered through the porous jar, which was wrapped in a cloth. In this way fresh water could be poured from the spout.'[47]

Although there were many public holidays and the streets were always particularly busy on Sundays, it was still rare in the nineteenth century for young girls to be allowed to attend public events. For this reason the drawing-rooms in their own homes were their most usual places of entertainment. In these large rooms, furnished for the purpose, wealthy families received visitors, conversed and danced. The more cultivated among them even organized literary evenings, some of which achieved great success at the time.

Although the large doors and windows encouraged freedom of movement between the rooms and linked the house with the outside world, they had an adverse effect on privacy. Various ways were found to deal with this problem. One was the introduction of *mamparas* or screen doors which were used to separate spaces from one another or at least to establish a visual barrier between rooms. They were much used and became a new decorative element for craftsmen to explore. Even when the large doors were open, the *mamparas* could be used when required.

However, the many large openings which encouraged the air to circulate posed other problems – they tended to let in too much light, and during heavy downpours water readily found its way in. Increasing use was made of *lucetas* (coloured glass panes) and wooden, louvred shutters. The spectacular *lucetas* were to be seen in all areas of the city, in both private houses and other

Early twentieth-century door-screen in the house of Regino Boti in Guantánamo. These doors are both functional and decorative and became an indispensable part of interiors at this time.

buildings – they were remarkably inventive and varied in design. They are in fact so decorative and specifically Cuban in character that it is easy to forget that their original purpose was strictly functional.

Apart from finding solutions to the practical problems associated with sunlight, ventilation and the use of space, the builders of Cuba's houses were concerned with decorative problems such as the treatment of the wall surfaces. As well as having a strong taste for architectural detail, local people had an undeniable fondness for what might be called 'chromatic eccentricity'. All the houses in Cuba were painted, the variety of colours being particularly marked in Havana itself: 'The walls of the houses, mansions and towers are painted in blue, yellow, green or orange, and are often decorated with frescoes. This is to counteract the blinding effect of bright sunlight on white painted walls.'[48]

Many drawing rooms also had decoratively painted dados. This form of decoration continued to be used for a long time but was eventually replaced with *azulejos* or ceramic tiles, which were not so easily damaged.

Walking through the arcades

Towards the end of the eighteenth century the town began to extend beyond the limits of the old walled area, but it was only in the nineteenth that Havana embarked upon a programme of major development there. In the early years of the century the rate of urban growth, high land values and lack of space in the inner city were increasingly marked. These were some of the factors which led to numerous building projects beyond the city walls. It was a process which was to last nearly the whole century and entailed considerable movement of population. The new overall town plan attempted an orderly approach to the inclusion of the outer zones and gave priority to projects in these areas. This vast urbanizing movement had a radical impact on the appearance of the town, now free to use all the space available for its development, while providing the Cuban house with ample scope to evolve in new ways.

By the eighteenth century arcades were being built on the street side of the houses situated around the main squares (similar to the arcades around the internal patios) for the benefit of pedestrians. This tradition was continued in the nineteenth-century developments outside the city walls, and was to become a characteristic feature of Cuban houses. In the provincial towns especially the arcades became one of the most important amenities in the social and family life of the neighbourhood. 'These outside corridors perform the same

Previous pages: Typical middle-class houses in the Calzada del Cerro in Havana, built at the end of the nineteenth century. They have a shared colonnade, large doors and window grilles. Individual touches are added by the use of a great variety of ornamental motifs.

Opposite: Ground floor of the house on the corner of Calle Mercaderes and Calle Obrapía in Havana. The ceiling and the classical mouldings date from the nineteenth century. Today the building houses a cultural institution, La Casa Simón Bolívar.

Opposite: The Palacio de Las Ursulinas in the Avenida de Bélgica, Havana. At the beginning of the twentieth century the incredible variety of arcades built along Havana's streets transformed the city's classical appearance, often with the eclectic results illustrated.

Below right: A house on El Malecón, Havana. The originality and imagination of Cuban builders at the beginning of the twentieth century ensured that every façade had an individual stamp. Architectural styles were freely adapted in this heterogeneous city.

function as the "fireside"[49] in English-speaking countries … – it is the place where people gather after their evening meal, where they meet to discuss local news and the latest scandal, where families discuss their most intimate concerns or where they consider questions of the day and politics.'[50]

All the buildings along the new streets and avenues were built with colonnades or individual porticoes, giving the city its own very characteristic appearance. Porticoes were to be seen everywhere in Havana, and the regulations for the city and surrounding areas even stipulated that they had to be included in all new buildings. The columns that thus became so typical led the novelist Alejo Carpentier to call Havana 'the city of a thousand columns'. At the beginning of the century this is how a traveller described the town: 'The streets are fine and wide; the buildings have echoes of an American style; the low houses with their arched windows and marble floors are elegantly furnished and lived in for the most part by country-born people and foreigners. These outer parts of the city have beautiful *paseos* … elegant avenues … wide carriageways … a magnificent theatre … and lastly the main factories and industrial buildings.'[51]

Most of the dwellings in the outlying areas of the city were still fairly plain in appearance, even when they had some of the characteristics of the typical Cuban house. Some contemporary accounts help to give an idea of what they were like: ' It is fair to say that the inhabitants live in the street. As the houses are primarily designed to let in as much air as possible, with the large doors opening directly on to the living room always open (there is no corridor in between) and the large, arched windows reaching almost from the ground to the roof, any passers-by are fully aware of everything happening inside; in the same way the youngest of the children is able to observe what is happening in the street ... .'[52]

Another account gives an equally clear picture of the houses of the middle classes: 'A pretty Cuban house, with its frescoed walls, its beautiful grilles, pilasters and decorative details, is a work of art of grace and beauty. The main door is very large in proportion to the rest of the building. Inside is the elegant *volanta*, which acts as the family's feet, as they nearly always use it when they venture out of their house.'[53]

The mansions outside the city walls

At the beginning of the nineteenth century the aristocracy still preferred to live in the old town, which continued by and large to be the case until the walls were demolished in 1865. This led to the immediate development of the surrounding area and the aristocrats gradually abandoned the old streets. In the new districts, just as in the old, the houses were mixed, but the properties that the very rich built for themselves were more luxurious than ever.

The first truly palatial mansion to be erected was the Palacio Aldama. Nothing built in the first half of the nineteenth century – not even some of the residences in the old city – was able to surpass its magnificence. Its owner, the powerful Don Domingo de Aldama, was intent on building the biggest mansion of its time and commissioned Don Manuel José Carrerá, one of the few professional architects then practising on the island, to carry out the task. Its splendour and the high quality of the workmanship matched the owner's immense fortune and the cultural sophistication of his family. His daughter was married to Domingo del Monte, a noted Creole intellectual (the most important literary salons of the time were held at their home).

Left: The ironwork on nineteenth-century buildings became more elaborate and lace-like. A fine example is this grille between the *zaguán* (vestibule) and the patio in the Palacio Aldama in the El Cerro district.

Below: Colonnade of the Casa de Cosme Blanco Herrera. Stone has taken the place of both wood and iron in the building of the balustrades.

Some time later, during the second half of the nineteenth century, other aristocrats followed the example of Aldama and built themselves new, grand homes near the site of the old walls, in an area where a few wealthy families were already living. These increasingly large mansions were usually designed by professional architects who, like Carrerá earlier, had made their reputation with government buildings in Havana. They made an equally impressive impact on the city when they built these huge private houses. The Palacio de la Marquesa de Balboa, the Palacio del Marqués de Villalba and the Balaguer residence are all particularly notable examples.

Nineteenth-century architecture is typified by the use of a neo-classical style, embellished with certain features necessitated by the demands of the climate and economic circumstances. New trends from Europe found their way to Cuba and were freely adapted, as often happens, using an almost casual selection of their ornamental details.

The luxury country villas

Yet another kind of house, crucial to the history of Cuban architecture, was built during the nineteenth century. The wealthiest families in Havana began to spend short periods outside the city when the weather was at its hottest, in order to get away from its suffocating atmosphere. The summer residence of the Captains-General – also known as the Quinta de los Molinos del Rey – was built for this purpose. It stands at the far end of the Tacón *paseo*, and its grounds originally extended from the Calzada de Infanta to the foot of the Castillo del Príncipe. Most of this land was separated from the house very early on and became part of Havana's Botanical Gardens. There are a number of statues in the luxuriantly planted gardens, prominently placed in little streams or on artificial rock pedestals. The two-storeyed house is built of wood and stone and roofed with tiles. The ground floor has an imposing arcade around all four sides. All the reception rooms are on this floor and the bedrooms are on the upper floor. Separated from the house and its garden were a number of outbuildings, used chiefly as accommodation for the carriage and living quarters for the servants. The style of the Quinta de los Molinos is reminiscent of the houses built in the country for the plantation owners.

Interestingly, this was not the area in which most of the rich people of Havana built their summer homes. They went a little further away from the centre of town to settle in the neighbouring district of El Cerro. The houses built here are markedly different from the Cuban houses so far described. Around 1840 the El Cerro district was established as the favourite holiday place for Havana's wealthiest residents. Their *quintas* or villas, with their grand porticoes and large gardens, line the main

Opposite: When the *quintas* of the El Cerro district were built, the traditional building plan was abandoned in favour of a new kind of house, surrounded by its garden and with external loggias. A fine example of the new style is the Casa de Cosme Blanco Herrera, No. 505 Calle Línea in the El Vedado district, built at the turn of the century. The ironwork of the garden grilles and the balustrades is outstanding.

Above: View of the extensive gardens, filled with statues and fountains, at the Quinta de los Molinos in Havana.

avenue in this exclusive area. When the old Creole aristocracy came to spend some time in their properties here they never missed an opportunity for sumptuous receptions, particularly if there were any important visitors to the capital. The large gardens and reception rooms were tailor-made for such social occasions.

These houses were built in a slightly more modern style than those in the old town or near the ramparts. Although they were used for only part of the year, visitors were invariably struck by their great beauty and luxury. Accounts by well-known travellers, such as José Jacinto Salas y Quiroga and the Rev. Abiel Abbott, give a good idea of life in El Cerro at the time: 'The resplendent *quintas* to be seen there excite the curiosity of the visitor. Particularly notable is the residence of the Conde de Villanueva, currently the Superintendent-General of Finances and the most influential and powerful person in his country. It is an extremely elegant house, well and lavishly built, with huge gardens planted with exotic trees and flowers. There are fountains and magnificent statues, iron and bronze grilles: everything contributes to a feast for the eyes. Not far away is the Conde Santovenia's villa, even more sumptuous and elegant, with its Greek portico. To its left is the residence of the Conde de Casa Lombillo. Overall, the whiteness of the houses and the green of the countryside amaze and enchant.'[54]

'The crowning pleasure of our morning walk was a visit to the mansion of the Conde Fernandino. It is a huge edifice, and his ancestral home. He has undertaken a programme of restoration work which has already cost one hundred thousand dollars. The reception rooms are spacious and elegant. His mother, the Condesa, and the Conde himself each have a suite of rooms for their own use. From the balcony of this superb residence one can clearly see the stables, where the horses are busy feeding.'[55]

These *quintas* became famous for the scale of their gardens, previously unknown in Cuba. Their size encouraged certain changes in lifestyle. For instance, it was now possible to build stabling and stores at the back of the house. The mansions on the outskirts of Havana, freed from the restricted space within the city walls, now had enough room to build an outside patio and plant a garden all round the house – of greater or lesser size, according to the resources and preferences of the owners. The gardens made it necessary to install grilles to mark their boundaries, and the wonderful filigrees designed by craftsmen for the purpose greatly added to the splendour and richness of these properties. This use of grilles was largely limited to the El Cerro district in the nineteenth century and continued in the El Vedado area for a little longer. Some of the finest examples of this work can be seen at the Country Club and on some of the houses at Miramar.

Cuban houses, even if they possess no garden or indoor patio, have always been adorned with plants and flowers. In the El Cerro district the

Opposite: The end of the colonial era coincided with a period of eclecticism in Cuban building. Various styles were freely adapted, but without abandoning any of the most important structural elements of colonial architecture.

loggias surrounding the *quintas*, rather like the indoor patios, played a special part in the life of the household. They were the place where members of the family got together and where the children often came to play.

The entrance led straight into enormous salons – firstly into a drawing-room, then into another cool, pleasant space that was used as a dining-room, beyond which was the patio. There were many big windows, just as in the grand houses close to the city walls, and all had grilles. Increasingly, wrought iron was used in a variety of ways to decorate the capital's houses and became an outstanding feature of their design.

Sometimes a wing was built at the back of the house to accommodate a kind of swimming pool or several marble bath-tubs. On particular days the men and the women of the house came separately to bathe there.

The residences in the El Cerro district represent one of the most important stages in the development of Cuban domestic architecture. It is characteristically Cuban that certain elements that are both functional and decorative – such as the coloured glass windows, the wrought-iron grilles and the *mamparas* or shutters – became prominent decorative features as a direct result of the ingenuity of Creole craftsmen, using new techniques that had been introduced into the island primarily for the development of certain industries.

After the success of this new district a similar holiday development was begun close to the sea in the El Vedado area. This project was abandoned, however, as a result of the events which overtook the country in the second decade of the twentieth century. Only a few houses were built there and these could not compare with the palatial dwellings at El Cerro.

The walls and ceilings of the Palacio Aldama in Havana are decorated with neo-classical landscapes, garlands and Pompeiian motifs, in keeping with the taste of the time.

An architecture in the spirit of the Cuban people

In tracing the history of the Cuban house we have been able to pick out its consistent features. These include a willingness to adapt to environmental conditions, a varied range of structural elements and a very pragmatic approach to the use of architectural systems and styles borrowed from other countries. Every detail illustrates the ingenuity of the builders and craftsmen, who were able to use their sources of inspiration and references as a starting point for a style of their own. Most of the characteristic elements of Cuban architecture were arrived at by balancing functional requirements with decorative ones. The interplay between architecture and the decorative arts was particularly productive, and the details of decoration became as important to the design as the overall structure of the building. The general effect of the Cuban colonial house is as pleasing as is its attention to the smallest detail.

Local considerations and the different ways of life of the island's inhabitants had a determining effect on how Cuban houses looked. The choice of materials they were built with had an equally important role in defining the architecture. For a long time the builders had to depend on what was available on the island to make balustrades, grilles or ceilings. Progress in industry and the development of techniques that could be adapted for use by craftsmen inevitably led to a new approach to house building. The first material to be used for all construction purposes had been wood. However, when the use of iron became widespread, it tended to be employed instead of wood for many architectural details. Once the craftsmen had mastered its technique, they were able to create a range of completely new forms

Left: Cárdenas was developed in the nineteenth century in the classical idiom then in fashion in Havana. There are many examples of local variants of neo-classicism in Cuba. Cárdenas' own rather severe appearance is attributable to the predominance of straight lines in the pilasters, cornices, mouldings and parapets on the façades.

Overleaf: Calle Obrapía in old Havana.

of ornamentation. These craftsmen showed unlimited imagination in their decorative schemes, which remains clearly visible today in many surviving nineteenth-century houses.

The development of house building (and architecture generally) had always depended on the skills of local builders. Until the middle of the nineteenth century they were artisans who learned on the job. In 1851 a School of Master Builders and Surveyors was founded, which led to some improvements in practice. The School began to train practitioners. They attained only a moderate standard, but were certainly better qualified than before. However, it was not until 1902 that the School of Engineers, Electricians and Architects was founded within the University of Havana, so that the first properly qualified architects could work on large-scale urban housing developments.

It is worth emphasizing that throughout the colonial period the island was quick to respond to influences from abroad and to absorb styles originating in Europe. The prevailing architectural language in 'the old continent' was adopted and modified in Cuba according to the knowledge, imagination and skill of the local builders.

The typical Cuban house built between the sixteenth and nineteenth centuries clearly demonstrates a continuous development in the creative process and accurately reflects the evolution of the lifestyle of the people who lived in these houses. Both Cuba's architecture and the people themselves have, throughout their history, shown an indomitable will to create an identity of their own.

195

Notes

1 For further information, see *La población de Cuba*, Centro de Estudios Demográficos.
2 Nicolás Guillén, 'La canción del bongó', in *Sóngoro Cosongo*, p. 12 (the bongo is an African drum used by Cuban blacks at celebrations).
3 Ignacio Urrutia y Montoya, *Teatro histórico, jurídico y político militar de la Isla de Fernandina*, p. 92.
4 Esquemeling, *Piratas de la América*, pp. 194–195.
5 Esquemeling, *op. cit.*, p. 196.
6 Irene Wright, *Historia documentada…*, p. 24.
7 *Five Diaries during the Siege of Havana*, p. 196.
8 The term *ingenio* is applied to both the sugar-cane fields and the sugar mills. *Cafetal* means coffee plantation.
9 José Jacinto Salas y Quiroga, *Viajes*, p. 22.
10 José Jacinto Salas y Quiroga, *op. cit.*, p. 46.
11 Nicolás Tanco Armero, *La Isla de Cuba*, in Juan Pérez de la Riva, *La Isla de Cuba en el siglo XIX vista por los extranjeros*, p. 110.
12 Samuel Hazard, *Cuba with Pen and Pencil*, 1871, p. 146.
13 Samuel Hazard, *op.cit.*, p. 146. According to him, *tasajo* was made with beef dried in the sun and salted. It was a popular dish and was even eaten by well-off families on days when they had no guests.
14 As previously noted, *ajiaco* was originally an Indian dish. At this period it was made with fresh beef or pork, many varieties of vegetables, maize and green

bananas. The resulting stew was thickened with a floury root called *malanga* and lemon juice was added as a final touch.
15 Frederika Bremer, *Letters from Cuba*, 1980, p. 101.
16 Richard Henry Dana, Jr., *Travels in Cuba*, 1860, quoted in Samuel Hazard, *op. cit.*, p. 235.
17 Richard Henry Dana, Jr., *op. cit.*, p. 231.
18 Frederika Bremer, *op. cit.*, p. 27.
19 Frederika Bremer, *op. cit.*, p. 28.
20 Frederika Bremer, *op. cit.*, p. 64.
21 Frederika Bremer, *op. cit.*, p. 64.
22 Abiel Abbott, *Letters*, 1965, p. 108.
23 Abiel Abbott, *op. cit.*, p. 108.
24 Roland T. Ely, *Cuban Merchants in the 19th Century*, p. 36.
25 Frederika Bremer, *op. cit.*, p. 51.
26 Frederika Bremer, *op. cit.*, p. 56.
27 Duvergier de Hauranne, *Cuba y las Antillas*, in Juan Pérez de la Riva, *op.cit.*, p. 160.
28 French phrase used in the Spanish text.
29 Duvergier de Hauranne, *Cuba y las Antillas*, in Juan Pérez de la Riva, *op. cit.*, p. 166.
30 H.B. Auchinloss, *La fabricación del azúcar*, in Juan Pérez de la Riva, *op. cit.*, pp. 200–203.
31 Frederika Bremer, *op. cit.*, p. 79.
32 Samuel Hazard, *op. cit.*, p. 140.
33 Francis Robert Jameson, *Cartas habaneras*, in Juan Pérez de la Riva, *op. cit.*, p. 48.

34 José Jacinto Salas y Quiroga, *op. cit.*, p. 33.
35 Frederika Bremer, *op. cit.*, p. 27.
36 Frederika Bremer, *op. cit.*, p. 18.
37 Alexander von Humboldt, *Essai politique sur l'île de Cuba*, p. 7.
38 Francis Robert Jameson, *Cartas habaneras*, in Juan Pérez de la Riva, *op. cit.*, p. 49.
39 Roland T. Ely, *op. cit.*, p. 35.
40 Frederika Bremer, *op. cit.*, p. 48.
41 Frederika Bremer, *op. cit.*, p. 47.
42 Frederika Bremer, *op. cit.*, p. 48.
43 Frederika Bremer, *op. cit.*, pp. 26–27.
44 Frederika Bremer, *op. cit.*, p. 29.
45 Frederika Bremer, *op. cit.*, p. 143.
46 Nicolás Tanco Armero, *La Isla de Cuba*, in Juan Pérez de la Riva, *op. cit.*, p. 114.
47 Frederika Bremer, *op. cit.*, p. 50.
48 Frederika Bremer, *op. cit.*, p. 27.
49 English word used in the Spanish text.
50 Nicolás Tanco Armero, *La Isla de Cuba*, in Juan Pérez de la Riva, *op. cit.*, p. 127.
51 Nicolás Tanco Armero, *La Isla de Cuba*, in Juan Pérez de la Riva, *op. cit.*, p. 110.
52 Nicolás Tanco Armero, *La Isla de Cuba*, in Juan Pérez de la Riva, *op. cit.*, p. 126.
53 Frederika Bremer, *op. cit.*, p. 140.
54 José Jacinto Salas y Quiroga, *op. cit.*, p. 80.
55 Abiel Abbott, *op. cit.*, p. 180.

Bibliography

Abbott, Abiel, *Cartas*, Editorial del Consejo Nacional de Cultura, Havana, 1965.

Balboa y Troa de Quesada, Silvestre de, *Espejo de Paciencia*, Biblioteca Básica de Literatura Cubana, Editorial Arte y Literatura Cubana, Havana, 1975.

Boti, Regino, *Poesía*, Letras Cubanas, Editorial Arte y Literatura, Instituto del Libro, Havana, 1977.

Bremer, Frederika, *Cartas desde Cuba*, Editorial Arte y Literatura, Havana, 1980.

Carrion, Miguel de, *Las Honradas*, Instituto Cubano del Libro, Havana, 1973.

Carrion, Miguel de, *Las Impuras*, Instituo Cubano del Libro, Havana, 1972.

Chateloin, Felicia, *La Habana de Tacón*, Letras Cubanas, Editorial Arte y Literatura, Instituto del Libro, Havana, 1989.

Cotarelo, Ramón, *Matanzas en su arquitectura*, Letras Cubanas, Editorial Arte y Literatura, Instituto del Libro, Havana, 1993.

Diaz Quiñones, Marino, 'La ciudad alegre y descuidada', *Sociedad Cubana de Ingenieros*, Havana, June 1917.

Esquemeling, *Piratas de la América*, Comisión Cubana de la Unesco, Havana, 1963.

García Santana, Alicia; Angelbello, Teresita; and Echeragusia, Victor, *Trinidad de Cuba*, Ediciones Abya-Yala, Ecuador, 1996.

González Díaz, Francisco, *Un canario en Cuba*, Imprenta La Prueba, Havana, 1916.

Goodman, Walter, *Un artista en Cuba*, Editorial del Consejo Nacional de Cultura, Havana, 1965.

Guillén, Nicolás, *Sóngoro Cosongo*, Editorial Losada, Buenos Aires, 1957.

Heredia, Nicolás, *Leonela*, Biblioteca Básica de Autores Cubanos, Instituto Cubano del Libro, Havana, 1972.

Humboldt, Alexander von, *Essai politique sur l'île de Cuba*, [1826], Nanterre, Editions Erasme, 1989.

La población de Cuba, Centro de Estudios Demográficos, Editorial de Ciencias Sociales, Havana, 1976.

Le Riverend, Julio, *La República, dependencia y revolución*, Editorial Pueblo y Educación, Havana, 1969.

Llanes, Llilian, *La Transformación de La Habana a través de la Arquitectura*, Editorial Letras Cubanas, Havana, 1993.

Llanes, Llilian, *Apuntes para una historia sobre los constructores cubanos*, Editorial Letras Cubanas, Havana, 1986.

Loveira, Carlos, *Generales y Doctores*, Instituto Cubano del Libro, Havana, 1972.

Mendéz Capote, Renée, *Memorias de una Cubanita que nació con el siglo*, Instituto Cubano del Libro, Havana, 1969.

Pérez de la Riva, Juan, *La Isla de Cuba en el siglo XIX vista por los extranjeros*, Editorial de Ciencias Sociales, Havana, 1981.

Pichardo, Hortensia, *Documentos para la historia de Cuba*, vol ii, Editorial de Ciencias Sociales, Havana, 1969.

Primelles, León, *Crónica cubana 1915–1918*, Editorial Lex, Havana, 1958.

Salas Quiroga, Jacinto, *Viajes*, Editorial del Consejo Nacional de Cultura, Havana, 1964.

Segre, Roberto, *La Vivienda en Cuba. República y Revolución*. Concurso 13 de marzo. University of Havana, 1985.

Venegas, Carlos, *La Urbanización de las murallas: dependencia y modernidad*, Letras Cubanas, Editorial Arte y Literatura, Instituto del Libro, Havana, 1990.

Vitier, Cintio, *Lo Cubano en la poesía*, Letras Cubanas, Editorial Arte y Literatura, Instituto del Libro, Havana, 1970.

Weiss, Joaquín, *La arquitectura colonial cubana*, Havana and Seville, 1996.

Index

Translated by Harriet Mason

First published in hardcover in the United States of America in 1999
by Thames & Hudson Inc., 500 Fifth Avenue, New York, New York 10110

First paperback edition 2001

Library of Congress Catalog Card Number 99-70935

ISBN 0-500-28272-2

Printed and bound in Italy